Hitler's French Volunteers

Hitler's French Volunteers

Christophe Léguerandais

Pen & Sword
MILITARY

First published in Great Britain in 2016 by
Pen & Sword Military
an imprint of
Pen & Sword Books Ltd
47 Church Street
Barnsley
South Yorkshire
S70 2AS

Copyright © Christophe Léguerandais 2016

ISBN 978 1 47385 656 1

Typeset in Ehrhardt by
Mac Style Ltd, Bridlington, East Yorkshire
Printed and bound by Replika Press Pvt. Ltd.

Pen & Sword Books Ltd incorporates the imprints of Pen & Sword Archaeology,
Atlas, Aviation, Battleground, Discovery, Family History, History, Maritime,
Military, Naval, Politics, Railways, Select, Transport, True Crime, and Fiction,
Frontline Books, Leo Cooper, Praetorian Press, Seaforth Publishing and
Wharncliffe.

For a complete list of Pen & Sword titles please contact
PEN & SWORD BOOKS LIMITED
47 Church Street, Barnsley, South Yorkshire, S70 2AS, England
E-mail: enquiries@pen-and-sword.co.uk
Website: www.pen-and-sword.co.uk

Contents

Introduction

After the launch of Operation Barbarossa in June 1941, in addition to those nations allied to Germany, tens of thousands of volunteers from other occupied countries flocked to join the various expeditionary forces in order to participate in what promised to be an epic fight. Although not willing to return to a state of war following its defeat the year before, France, which had seen a large part of its territory invaded, now witnessed the birth of the so-called *Légion des volontaires français* (LVF) [Legion of French Volunteers]. The organisation was set up with the help of the German ambassador in Paris, with the aim of fighting on what was soon to become the Eastern Front. With the conviction that they were protecting their homeland from the threat of Bolshevism, many of the volunteers came from political parties that had sided with the Germans. Following an agreement with Hitler, units were formed of volunteers from the so-called 'non-German' countries, while those from 'Germanic' countries joined the Waffen SS.

From 1942 onwards, many wounded or reformed veterans decided to continue the fight and push their physical limits by joining the ranks of these various auxiliary groups, which were also open to younger recruits with no previous front-line experience. Indeed, despite Hitler's invasion of his enemy's land [Russia], many areas behind the front-line were still far from being pacified, forcing him to send new units to these areas to carry out such a task. The lengthening lines of communication in the East and Rommel's African Front meant that Hitler was seriously struggling from a lack of man-power. This was to be filled, in part, by a massive recruitment of foreign labour, which was ready to flock to his banner and serve him in his propaganda war.

The commitments in the East meant a compulsory labour service was officially established in Germany, and the competition between the various paramilitary units to recruit on its behalf was fierce. The LVF was too politicised and had too much 'French spirit' for some. It was shunned by many young men, who preferred to admire the troops in their silver runes, which they saw as being more of an elite army facing down this 'European creation'. In July 1943 they were finally allowed to join the SS, although not everyone was willing to go to the East to defend his ideals. After the defeat at Stalingrad, the decline of the Afrika Korps and the Battle of Kursk, the

Wehrmacht was facing retreat on all fronts. There were those who believed that the struggle against anti-communism must now take place on home soil with the help of pro-German organisations.

According to Reichsführer Himmler, these foreign fighters against Bolshevism were more 'trustworthy', as they were made up of volunteers with a common ideal and following his numerous requests to Hitler that they be incorporated into his SS, his wishes finally came true in 1944. Amalgamated into a single unit that would fight on foreign soil until the last day of the war, these Frenchmen in German uniforms would follow the oath that they had sworn until its conclusion.

This book is not a history of French collaboration, but a representation of the main units in which around 15,000 men fought side-by-side with the military forces of the Third Reich. It is not about Alsace-Lorraine, the region attached to Germany, which consequently saw many young Frenchmen forced into the different branches of the German Army and who were to suffer heavy losses on the Eastern Front. Nor is it

Frenchmen in French uniform speaking with German soldiers, one of whom is a member of the RAD. They wear white armbands on their left arm proclaiming '*Im Dienste der deutschen Wehrmacht*' [In Service of the German Army], indicating that they are attached to a German unit. The man in the centre has been discharged from the LVF and has been decorated with the *Croix de guerre légionnaire*.

about the French who fought with Mussolini, or those who were incorporated into Colonel Skorzeny's Brandenburg German Special Forces unit. The same goes for those working in France as members of the *Hilfpolizei* (auxiliary police), as interpretors for the *Kommandanturs* and *Feldgendarmerie*, the secretaries at the recruitment offices or various German departments (SiPo, SD, etc.) as well as the numerous plain-clothed agents working for the *Abwehr* [German military intelligence organisation].

Chapter One

The Legion of French Volunteers Against Bolshevism (LVF)

The LVF was created in Paris after being approved by Adolf Hitler in the summer of 1941, on the condition that the initiative would follow the collaborationist pro-German political parties, with no commitment to the French government, who instead preferred to keep its distance. These political groups were entrusted with recruiting volunteers for a new regiment in the German Army that was to fight in Russia. At the same time, anti-Communist White Russians arrived en masse from their motherland with the aim of fighting the Bolshevist Red Army.

The Deba camp near Krakow, in occupied Poland, was the chosen location for the training of the officially named *Französischer Infanterie-Regiment 638*, commanded by the French Colonel, Roger Labonne. The first contingent of 803 men and 25 officers arrived on 8 September 1941 to form the 1st Battalion, but a surprise awaited them; they learnt that they would have to fight whilst wearing a German Army uniform, the same uniform they had been fighting against for the past year and not the French Army uniform that had been promised them when they signed up. France was not at war with Russia and consequently the Hague Convention forbade them from fighting in their national uniform. This clause likewise affected the Spanish, Belgians, Danish and Dutch, who were also involved in the same struggle. A concession was made allowing them to wear a tricolour cloth badge on the right sleeve of their field uniform, thus distinguishing them from other soldiers. A second contingent of nearly 800 volunteers arrived on 20 September to form the 2nd Battalion. On 5 October the recruits were faced with a new challenge; they had to swear an oath of loyalty to Adolf Hitler, as was usual practice for the German Army. After several weeks of training, the 1st and 2nd Battalions set off for the front at the end of October. The legionnaires, divided into fourteen companies under the command of French officers, retained their flag and the use of weapons currently used by the French Army. By late November they were attached to the 7th Division of the 7th Bavarian Infantry Corps, commanded by General von Gablenz, and found themselves in the front-line facing the 32nd Siberian Division, near Djukowo, 70km from Moscow. Despite the exceptional cold and fatigue caused by severe hunger, they fulfilled their mission and were replaced by a German unit in early December. Nevertheless, a reorganisation of the unit was needed as a result of the missing, and dead, soldiers, as well as the incompetence that had been revealed at several levels, including management. A severe purge was carried out at the Kruszyna camp, in the General Government of Poland, and many 'political' soldiers took the opportunity to discharge themselves from the army and fight for their homeland once more. The 2nd Battalion was disbanded with all the men being put into the 1st Battalion and training began from scratch. Meanwhile, a third battalion had been in training at Deba since December 1941, and during all the years of its existence, the legion in the East would regularly receive new recruits from France.

In spring 1942 the two battalions of the LVF (1st and 3rd) were assigned to the Army Group Centre in the Steppes, although they were curiously sent to two different locations and therefore operated separately. From now on, the 'Great Front' was at an end and now their task was to fight the partisans behind the Reich forces. Meanwhile in France, the government carried out various upheavals to the LVF, including renaming it the Tricolour Regiment, but after initial success, the operation was denied by Hitler and it ended in failure. The volunteers in the East were not affected by these changes and were more preoccupied with the dangers that surrounded them, rather than what was happening at home. They witnessed the arrival of new comrades, including officers, who thanks to their previous military experience, were now put at the service of the Legion.

Since early 1943 the French government had funded an intense propaganda programme using meetings, posters and other publications to recruit new members to make up for the losses incurred. From its creation, some members of the Legion had seen their windows smashed by opponents to the new order, and those on leave often found themselves targets of snipers or attacks. The general public were more concerned with finding food to eat for themselves, rather than worrying about the fate of their sons in the land of Stalin. In October one of the most important figures in the story of the French volunteers, Colonel Edgar Puaud, arrived in Russia. As head of the entire Legion, his aim was to bring together the 1st and 3rd Battalions, who at this point were still fighting separately. He also started to put together a new 2nd Battalion which was to be attached to the other two, straddling the main road between Moscow and Minsk, in Belarus. However, the three battalions were still understaffed.

1944 was a turning point for the LVF, after the French *maquis* [rural guerilla band of French Resistance fighters] began to intensify their operations and a deal was made to combat the so-called 'terrorists' (supporters of General de Gaulle, who had been living in exile in London since 1940, communists, apolitical resistors etc.). In the East, the LVF continued to fight the Soviet partisans behind the 4th German Army, but by late June its fate had been decided; it was to return to France. A few hours before its departure, the Legion was gathered in the village of Bobr, near Berezina, when a counter-order arrived. Operation Bagration, in which 193 Russian divisions had launched an assault on 'Fortress Europe' in a gigantic offensive that was to sweep the Wehrmacht, had begun on 23 June. The legionnaires were now trusted with delaying the Soviets' advance so that the German units who had been dispersed by the violence and speed of the attack would have a chance to regroup. The 1st and 3rd battalions were expected to stay put and hold their positions with just over 400 men. Assisted by an SS-Polizei unit and five Tiger tanks, they took up their position on a strategic bridge to stop the enemy from crossing, but instead of partisans, they now found themselves facing the Red Army. For forty-eight hours, one Russian attack after another was repelled, as the Tigers destroyed their tanks and the legionnaires pushed back the infantry. On the morning of 27 June, the French were relieved by another German unit, which would later be completely wiped out. Between forty and fifty enemy tanks (T34s and American Shermans) were destroyed during the fierce fighting. Soviet radio announced in a statement that units of the 2nd White Russian Front had run into resistance from two French divisions for forty-eight hours. For its part, the LVF, which had suffered around forty fatalities, began its retreat after the collapse of the Army Group Centre, the fate of which was linked to that of the rest of the German Army.

Now removed from the Eastern Front, the survivors from the fighting in Russia were grouped together at the Greifenberg Barracks, the LVF's main base in Germany. Its depleted numbers were reinforced with new arrivals, volunteers who had served in other German units, loners arriving from Russia and soldiers returning from leave. By this time, large areas of France had been liberated following the Allied landings in Normandy on 6 June. For those soldiers far from home, no news of what had happened to their families was a blow to morale. Late August finally saw the departure for the SS training camp at Konitz, in northern Poland. The higher powers had decided that a new French SS brigade would be created and Himmler now declared that foreign volunteers would be poured into the Waffen SS. The last French unit to have fought on Russian soil was disbanded in order to form a new Waffen SS, who would train with their comrades from the SS-Freiwilligen-Sturmbrigade, as well as those who had been integrated into other German units. Unlike the officers, the plain legionnaires did not have a choice in the matter. Some of them refused on ideological or religious grounds, or by stating that they had signed a contract with the LVF, not the SS. These men were sent to concentration camps, where they would find fellow Waffen SS soldiers who had been sent there for indiscipline, dissent etc. Others would follow them there after a purge was carried out intending to keep only the best soldiers for this future SS division. The legionnaires in this division now had the benefit of three years combat experience, although many would fall in battle in Pomerania in early 1945, whilst others would end up in Berlin, defending Hitler in his bunker until the last days of the war. For many however, their last days were to be spent in captivity in the Soviet Union.

The entrance to the Borgnis-Desbordes barracks in Versailles. This photograph was taken on 27 August 1941, the first day volunteers were allowed to register. A ceremony was held involving many Franco-German officials, including Rudolf Schleier, who represented the German Ambassador to Vichy France, Otto Abetz. Schleier is in the centre of the photograph, with the white hair, wearing a dark suit. He is standing slightly in front of Pierre Laval, the future head of the French government. This was the first time the tricolour flag had been flown from any barracks in the occupied zone since the defeat of France the year before. After a brief ceremony on 3 September when the LVF received its own standard, the first troop contingent left Versailles the following day, bound for the East.

26 October 1941. Ambassador Fernand de Brinon (far left) attends a training exercise at Camp Deba, in occupied Poland, as a new 37mm Pak 36 anti-tank gun is commissioned into the 14th Company. Although the LVF was not technically controlled by the French state itself, the government still kept an eye on those men who were representing their country in the East. Several German officers, NCOs and interpretors are also watching this demonstration.

On their way to the front from Deba, the Legion arrived in Smolensk at the beginning of November 1941, where these bicycle liaison officers were photographed. The city lies partly in ruins as a result of earlier fighting in the summer. The men had to endure a very long and painful march of over 200km on foot through the snowy landscape, before continuing their journey by truck to the combat zone. Hundreds of men either got lost or were sent home ill, mainly as a result of the climatic conditions. The propaganda machine presented them as pioneers in a crusade that France must fight in, in order to deserve its place in the Europe of tomorrow.

A photograph taken by photo-journalist Ernst Gebauer, a corporal in propaganda company 694. It shows the driver of a 2nd Company infantry buggy just after the retreat in mid-December 1941. The Legion was a horse-drawn unit, with horses originally supplied by the Germans. Note that there is no tricolour on the right of his helmet (where you would normally find German insignia), as these were only supplied in small quantities.

3 March 1942, Camp Kruszyna. An honour guard during a ceremony in which the first Iron Crosses were handed out to deserving legionnaires, following their actions in December 1941.

3 March 1942, Camp Kruszyna. Second Lieutenant Pernel is decorated with the Iron Cross 2nd Class. As is tradition, he is not wearing a coat, despite the freezing weather. The award is presented by Army General, Baron Kurt Ludwig von Gienanth, Military Commander of the General Government.

3 March 1942, Camp Kruszyna. Legionary second class Jean Vilard is greeted by his friends shortly after receiving one of the five Iron Crosses to be handed out that day. He had been serving in Breslau, Silesia, since January and received his medal from Baron Kurt Ludwig von Gienanth. Three other Iron Cross 2nd class medals were awarded to soldiers who had distinguished themselves during December 1941, but were hospitalised at the time of the ceremony.

Colonel Roger Labonne, wearing his Iron Cross 2nd Class awarded on 3 March 1942, is seated next to Cavalry General Baron Kurt Ludwig von Gienanth at a celebration to mark the event.

27 March 1942. The LVF head office is inaugurated in the presence of (L to R); Battalion Chief André Girardeau and Colonel Labonne, who had both returned to France at the time. On the far right is Julius Westrick, advisor to the German Ambassador Otto Abetz.

Two officers responding to questions from a journalist on Radio-Paris.

On 2 April 1942 the first soldiers returned home from the Eastern Front on leave. Here they are being taken to the Queen's Barracks, Versailles, which had been the LVF's headquarters since December 1941. It was previously the Borgnis-Desbordes Barracks.

Legionnaires photographed eating in the Queens' Barracks on 2 April 1942. As you can tell by their 'older' faces, married men or fathers were given priority when it came to being granted leave.

The 3rd Battalion leaves Camp Deba by rail in May 1942, heading for the combat zone in central Russia, south-east of Smolensk.

A train carrying soldiers of the 3rd Battalion stops on its way to the front, under the watchful eye of Colonel Albert Ducrot. He had received the Legion's first standard in Versailles, on 3 September 1941 and was later replaced by Captain André Demessine, on 7 June 1942.

Colonel Ducrot (right) in May 1942, just after the arrival of the 3rd Battalion in his sector. It was attached to the 221 Security Division and went into the lines in the Cholmy then Gomel districts. Note the insignia visible in the bottom left, comprised of a rectangle. This signified an infantry unit.

Lieutenant Maurice Berret of 10th Company, surrounded by his men in May 1942. Each company was divided into several sections that occupied different positions in different villages. In each of these villages the men had to build bunkers to protect the operations base, once the section chiefs had decided where it would be. Contact with the natives was very agreeable. Once the command posts had been set up, each group and section started its surveillance missions: patrols combed the forests and night raids were carried out on potential suspects, with everyone looking to take the first shot.

Commander Max Lelongt (right), head doctor of 3rd Battalion sharing a drink with his comrades in late spring, 1942. Legionnaire Krisrovieks (centre) would be killed the following year. They were fighting the partisans, or 'bandits' according to the official terminology; a mixture of Red Army troops encircled by the German offensive, and locally recruited peasants. Both were familiar with the terrain and were often helped by the local peasants, who were caught between the two sides. Men and equipment were also parachuted in to boost the regular forces.

Sergeant (nurse) Etienne Gérard being buried by the unit chaplain, Monseigneur Mayol Lupé (right). Gérard was a member of the 3rd Battalion and was killed after being crushed by a car, on May 22 1942.

A legionnaire poses for a press photographer in spring 1942.

Sonderführer (Z) Gérald de Baecker (far right) delivering a report on the 3rd Battalion in May 1942. The report would be published in the various French newspapers de Baecker worked for.

The legionnaires were confronted with vast areas that they had to pacify. The enemy was elusive, always managing to slip away, except when they were outnumbered, and their main targets were the supply lines leading to the German front lines. Massive operations were planned to encircle the partisans, with the help of the Germans and aided by the *Ostruppen*, the anti-Communist Russian volunteers who fought for Germany. Due to lack of funds, the enemy was often able to escape and regroup and although there was some success (prisoners taken, weapons seized etc.), it was a never ending struggle.

Captain André Demessine, commander of 11th Company, surrounded by his men. June 1942.

Legionnaires with a Panzer IV tank of the 19th Panzer-Division, during an operation carried out in the 221 Security Division's sector, June 1942.

29 May 1942. The latest soldiers to be given leave seen here in the Queen's Barracks canteen, Versailles.

29 May 1942. As the latest soldiers on leave arrive, they observe their future comrades as they march through the streets of Versailles. Amongst them, on the lower-right, is a West-Indian soldier, one of a few who served in the Legion. Hauptmann Treffert, commander of the *Deutsche Sonderstab bei der Frz. Legion* (the German Special Staff Officer to the French Legion) can be seen in the background on the right, recognizable by his slim physique.

Early June 1942. Soldiers on leave lay a wreath at the Tomb of the Unknown Soldier in Paris. They are led by Captain Château (seen on the left in Image 27, without a belt).

Spring 1942, Kruszyna Camp, near Radom. A military parade during the visit of the Legion chaplain, Monseigneur de Mayol de Lupé. The standard is held by Raymond Jeanvoine, one of the five men awarded the Iron Cross 2nd Class on 3 March.

An outside meal in the Legion's camp. Spring 1942.

Bolotowa, 16 June 1942. Colonel Weimann, the Regimental Group Commander, attached to the 3rd Battalion from 30 May to 17 June, presents five Iron Cross 2nd Class awards. Three recipients can be seen here: (L to R) Monseigneur Mayol de Lupé, Doctor Molinié and Captain André Demessine, the latter two were part of 11th Company.

Under the command of Captain Max Château, seen here wearing his officer's dagger, the first contingent of reinforcements gather in the courtyard of the Queen's Barracks. They would leave the barracks on 18 June 1942 and travel by train to Kruszyna, arriving on 22 June. The band that accompanied them to the station can be seen on the left.

Some of the 220 new recruits that made up the first contingent of reinforcements, now officially called the 1st Reinforcements.

Soldiers sing patriotic songs at Versailles train station on 18 June, shortly before heading to the Eastern Front.

Captain Château (still without a belt) and Commander Lacroix visiting injured soldiers in the French hospital at Suresnes, on 27 June 1942.

Invitation to an event in aid of the LVF, held on 12 July 1942 and organised by the City of Nantes Collaborative Group, who have put their official stamp in the bottom-right corner. The invitation declares that the event is held under the patronage of both the French and German authorities, and includes attractions such as a German military band, pastries and beer.

Vol.
au dos

DIE GRUPPE "**COLLABORATION**" VON NANTES
LADET EIN ZUR KIRMES - BAZAR

AM SONNTAG, 12. JULI
VON 14 BIS 19 UHR IN NANTES, PARK CHAVAGNES

11 Rue Mondésir Ecke Boulevard Delorme

zu Gunsten der L. V. F.
Franzoesische Freiwilligenlegion zum Kampf gegen den Bolschewismus
UNTER DER SCHIRMHERRSCHAFT DER DEUTSCHEN
UND FRANZOESISCHEN BEHOERDEN

ZAHLEREICHE DARBIETUNGEN UND UBERRASCHUNGEN
——— ORCHESTER — ZAUBERKUENSTLER u.s.w. ———
———— VERKAUFSTAENDE : BACKEREI, FRUECHTE
SCHOKOLADE — WEIN — BIER — PFANNKUCHEN u.s.w.

Eintritt : 1 fr.

Selected soldiers receiving the new medal, la *Croix de guerre légionnaire*, at a ceremony on 12 July 1942, the first anniversary of the LVF's creation, at the famous Hôtel des Invalides, Paris. By this time the LVF had officially been renamed the Tricolour Legion, however, it is clear from the soldiers' uniform that they earned their awards as members of the LVF, not the Tricolour Legion.

A poster using the theme of a crusade and showing the various participating countries. The knight's shield on the right, is a symbol of the anti-Bolshevik Legion.

Late 1942. The entrance to a cemetery in Smorki where legionnaires from 1st Battalion, who died fighting the partisans, are buried. The first legionnaire was buried here on 8 October 1941 and there were seventy-five graves here less than two years later. The inscription reads: 'To our dead who died for the new Europe'. The cemetery for 3rd Battalion was in Barysaw.

A member of 3rd Battalion carrying out a patrol by sleigh, during winter operations in early 1943.

A legionnaire is immortalised on film in a photograph taken by one of his comrades. Winter, early 1943.

Propaganda posters covered many walls in France, encouraging the population to join the unit.

Members of the LVF Veterans Association during a parade. The two legionnaires carrying the wreath are wearing the ribbon of the Iron Cross 2nd Class. A club for LVF veterans was opened in Paris on 29 July 1943. It was run by Guy Servant, who had fought during the first winter campaign.

Aspiring students at the LVF Cadet School in Guéret, learning how to handle weapons. In this case, a Schmeisser MP-28/II. The instructor's rank can be seen on his right sleeve. Note the different types of insignia worn by the soldiers on the right. As of 11 February 1943, volunteers were tenured to the ranks of the French Army and this fresh supply of 'quality' recruits, was an important asset for the future of the Legion.

Students from the LVF Cadet School parade past the Park Hotel [seat of the French Government], Vichy on 4 May 1943.

Men of 1st Company, 1st Battalion in Denisowitschi, June 1943. (L to R) Sergeants Girod, Paul Herbeck and Senouque. The latter would be killed in January 1944. 1st Battalion returned to Russia at the end of July 1942, having left Kruszyna on the 17th. Landing at Barysaw, it was attached to the 286th Security Division. Like their compatriots of 3rd Battalion, the legionnaires participated in operations against the partisans before retiring to the Smorki district (east of Barysaw) where they would remain until March 1944. Protecting the railway and the main road to Moscow would become their main priority.

French Ambassador Fernand de Brinon arrives at the Berezina river in June 1943, next to where the bridges were built for the Grand Army. Coincidentally, he is wearing the Imperial Eagle, inspired by the Napoleonic era. De Brinon is inspecting 1st Battalion, accompanied by Colonel Puaud (in French uniform), who can be seen hidden just behind his right shoulder.

Watched by members of the PK, Ambassador Fernand de Brinon, accompanied by Colonel Puaud, decorates legionnaires of 1st Battalion fighting in the East.

The fabric national badge that the French volunteers stitched on to the right sleeve of their uniform.

Late June 1943. A war correspondent team comprised of three German cameramen and SS-Kriegsberichter [war reporter] Weis, interviewing the men of 3rd Battalion for their story. On the right, a Waffen SS officer in glasses surveys the scene, while Second Lieutenant Seveau (with his back to the camera), asks an old peasant man some questions. Next to him is Lieutenant Audibert, with his serial number (638) on his epaulette. The two men were in charge of defending their position next to a tributary of the Dnieper, which included a bridge around 10km to the left of Mogilev, Belarus, before moving further west when they were attached to 11th Company. Following the German *Jagzug* model, at the end of October Lieutenant Seveau created an independent section that followed the Soviet method of laying mines to combat the enemy. This meant that advance patrols had to go out either early in the morning or late in the evening, taking routes that had to be changed at the last minute, so as not to reveal the final destination, in the hope of encircling the pockets of Soviet resistance. Using smaller weapons in order to move more quickly and silently, the aim of these expeditions was to discourage the partisans from occupying the surrounding villages, which they used as staging posts to ambush the French soldiers and move them into more rural areas.

Behind the front lines, the Steppes area where the Army Group Centre operated was infested with Soviet partisans. Here, a Russian old enough to bear arms is questioned by a legionnaire; you can see the embroidered LVF badge on his right sleeve. The ammunition belt of 100 MG34 cartridges is worn around the shoulders.

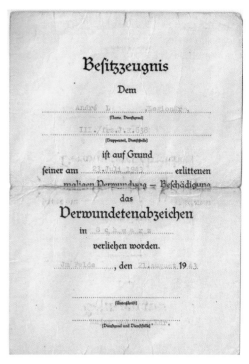

Document dated 21 August 1943 showing that volunteer André L. was awarded the German Wound Badge (black). This was a military decoration awarded to wounded soldiers of the German Army. The 'black, 3rd class' award was for those wounded once or twice by enemy action. He signed up on 27 July 1942 at Versailles and was given the serial number 7894. Sent to Kruszyna on 8 October, he was assigned to 3rd Battalion Headquarters on 8 January 1943.

The flag of the 1st regiment of the LVF and its guard of honour, at the Hôtel des Invalides, Paris, commemorating the second anniversary of the LVF, on 27 August 1943. General Bridoux had presented the flag in the name of France a little earlier, to Commander Demessine. On the left, an NCO carries certificates to be given to the families of those men who had died on the battlefield.

Under the gaze of the soldiers, the ceremony comprised of decorating wounded legionnaires, those who had been transferred to other German units, those still with the LVF and the parents of those who had shed their blood for the cause.

The flag of the Legion and its guard of honour about to leave the Place de l'Etoile, Paris, on 27 August 1943.

27 August 1943. After a ceremony at the Arc de Triomphe, where a wreath was laid on the Tomb of the Unknown Soldier, the standard and its guard of honour return to their billets. They are followed by other combatants who had fought in the East, cheered by crowds on both sides of the Champs-Elysées.

A small silver lapel pin worn by the civilian members of the 'Friends of the LVF'. The same insignia was also worn by veterans, although this had crossed swords behind a golden eagle.

Dressed in civilian clothing, Commander Demessine greets the legionnaires leaving Paris for the East, on 4 October 1943. Note that the volunteers do not wear the eagle bust on their uniforms, but some of them are wearing beautiful combat ribbons.

1 December 1943. Members of the LVF Veterans Association form a guard of honour outside Notre-Dame-des-Victoires church, Paris, after a Mass held in memory of the first legionnaires who had died during the fighting in December 1941. They are wearing the association uniform of black trousers, white shirt, black tie and a red armband bearing the imperial eagle and two swords. On the right is the German adviser, Julius Westrick.

Travel pass to Barysaw for a member of 1st Battalion, issued on 13 December 1943.

Front cover of one of the many flyers produced containing information about the terms of enlistment and the benefits of doing do.

One of the five 'Borodino' propaganda postcards representing the volunteers fighting in Russia, issued on 20 April 1942. Produced by the legion's head office, there was no need to use a stamp on the cards as the legionnaires were given the status of soldiers.

The mail delivery raises smiles at the Legion's barracks in Versailles. Spring 1944.

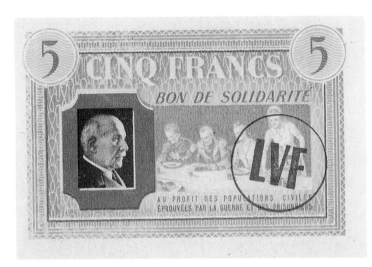

A public solidarity bond, the money from which supposedly went to civilian victims of the war, as well as prisoners in the German Stalags and Oflags. By stamping it, the LVF showed that they wanted to be associated with the operation.

The Legion often used Marshal Pétain as part of their propaganda, thanks to the place he held in the hearts of the French population. The main purpose of the LVF Association was to recruit volunteers for German Army units on the so-called Eastern Front, using various forms of propaganda, including meetings, posters, leaflets etc.

Chapter Two

The Tricolour Regiment

On his return as head of the French government in the spring of 1942, Pierre Laval instructed his Secretary of State, Jacques Benoist-Méchin, to examine the possibility of taking over the existing LVF, but give it a new role. The idea was to absorb the Legion into a new unit, which would be engaged in theatres of operation where French interests, as well as those of its colonial Empire, were involved. It would be a part of the French Army, under the direction of General Bridoux, the Secretary of State for War.

On 22 June 1942, the first anniversary of Operation Barbarossa, the central committee dissolved the LVF and renamed it the *Légion tricolore* (Tricolour Regiment). As well as a name change, there was also a personnel change in its 173 recruitment offices, and new faces appeared on its central committee. As well as fighting in the East, the Legion would now also fight in North Africa and other areas where the French Empire was threatened. Not only did this legitimisation mean that the Legion now found itself committed to several new engagements, most importantly it meant an influx of new professional soldiers. The unit was open to those serving in Vichy's *Armée d'Armistice* and those serving in North Africa and recruits were chosen from men who wanted to fight, but who shared the views of Marshal Pétain, and not the party leaders who advocated collaboration. Prisoners were still not allowed to serve, but the prospectus declared that those born in France, were naturalised foreigners or were natives of North Africa, could join. Nothing was left to chance; there were ceremonies, parades, the creation of a new medal (*la Croix de guerre légionnaire*), a new emblem and even the taking over of social services to highlight the benefits of volunteering.

Despite the success of the operation, Hitler and the Wehrmacht high commanders refused to recognise the Tricolour Regiment and only accepted the LVF, which they did not want to see removed in favour of a new unit that they mistrusted. They feared that the Tricolour Regiment would lead to a larger French Army than the one agreed on in the Armistice, and one that might someday even turn against them. Benoist-Méchin resigned on 9 October 1942 having been excluded from the Government. The Anglo-Americans landed on the north African coast the following month and a unit christened the African Phalanx was set up by the government, which operated in the same spirit as the Tricolour Regiment. The government issued press releases inviting volunteers to sign up and work in its departmental offices, which would be directed from its assembly centre in Guéret. In the end only a few officers from the Tricolour Regiment participated in this new project after being sent to Tunisia.

Without completely abandoning the goals of the Tricolour Regiment, it was eventually dissolved by the government after a law enacted on 28 December 1942. Its resources were then divided between the recovering LVF and the African Phalanx.

Late June 1942. At the headquarters of the anti-Bolshevik Legion in Paris, the government delegate, Jacques Benoist-Méchin (centre, below the portrait of Marshal Pétain), reveals the aims of the new Tricolour Regiment. The French government took over the LVF, renamed it and made it the basis of a new regiment. Once transformed, it was granted special benefits thanks to its 'official' recognition and there was even talk about the formation of an aviation section within the Tricolour Regiment. It's official hymn was La Marche Consulaire (Consular March).

In mid-July, the president of the Legion's management committee visited some of the injured LVF men in Suresnes hospital. He was accompanied by journalists as well as the German Ambassador's adviser, Julius Westrick, easily recognisable by his white hair.

Guéret, 25 August 1942. Under the watchful eye of the crowd, the first volunteers from the Free Zone are inspected by Jacques Benoist-Méchin (centre), Colonel Edgar Puaud and General Galy (right). Colonel Puaud was in command of the new legion. A career soldier, he had been a captain during the Great War and then assigned to the colonies, before taking responsibility for the Tricolour Regiment. After it was disbanded, he became the deputy military leader of the LVF. He was awarded the *Commandeur de la Légion d'honneur* on 8 April 1944 and promoted to brigadier. He ended the war as an Oberführer, the Waffen SS equivalent of brigadier.

The first volunteers in Guéret, 25 August 1942. Their motto was 'Plus est en nous' [There is more in us]. They were aware that following the amendments to the statutes of the Legion, they may be required to fight not just Bolshevism, but also its allies. Indeed, the *Französischer Infanterie-Regiment 638,* which had two battalions in training in Poland and behind the eastern frontlines would only fight against this one enemy. The new law enacted on 18 July worked in the Regiment's favour, as it meant that French laws would be applied to how medals were awarded (*Légion d'honneur,* Military Medal), how pay was received, what leave was granted, disability pensions, widow's pensions awarded etc. Professional soldiers would also benefit from taking part in the campaign, receiving promotions, citations etc.

Augustine Barracks, Guéret, 25 August. The Secretary of State, Jacques Benoist-Méchin, seen here dressed in black, converses with Colonel Puaud, on his right. Benoist-Méchin was on the Central Committee, which now included civil authorities, as well as religious, military and other government members. On his left is the Prefect of the Creuse department [the area in which the barracks were located], and General Galy, Commissioner General of the Tricolour Regiment.

Above and Opposite: The men parade after the ceremony, led by Jean Boudet-Gheusi (on the right, wearing glasses). He had joined on 25 June 1941 and would surrender in April 1945, whilst wearing the uniform of the Waffen SS Charlemagne Division.

The entrance to the Augustine barracks in Guéret. Commanded by Colonel Puaud, the men are dressed in their khaki uniforms – the German field grey uniform was only expected to be worn during operations. The authorisation to wear the French helmet, even in combat, was still on hold, as despite everything the German authorities had still not given its backing to the new legion. What's more, the German military authorities had refused to provide the necessary weapons to train the volunteers, who were becoming increasingly impatient as the fighting increased.

For two months the propaganda machine had been in full flow, printing brochures and launching a massive poster campaign, not to mention a daily radio show directed by the future SS Untersturmführer, Léon Gaultier. The legionnaires from Guéret participated in the ceremony, held in Paris, to mark the first anniversary of the creation of the anti-Bolshevik Legion. Having received their embroidered eagle badge the day before, they are seen here in front of Notre-Dame Cathedral, where a service was held to remember those who had fallen on the Eastern Front. The Bonapartist Benoist-Mechin believed that the volunteers' eagle brought to mind the Imperial eagle of Emperor Napoleon's armies.

Legionnaires, dressed in French khaki, in front of Notre-Dame Cathedral on their way to the Hôtel des Invalides, as part of the celebrations marking the unit's first anniversary on 27 August.

The first small contingent of volunteers march through the streets of Paris to the ceremony. 27 August 1942.

The well-known figures attending the ceremony in the courtyard of the Hôtel des Invalides, including (front row, R to L), Colonel Puaud, German Ambassador Otto Abtez, General Galy, Admiral Platon (representing Marshal Pétain), French Ambassador Fernand de Brinon (representing Pierre Laval) and Secretary of State Jacques Benoist-Méchin.

The standards for the future battalions presented by their commander, Colonel Puaud, during the ceremonial parade in the courtyard of the Hôtel des Invalides.

Leaving the Hôtel des Invalides after the ceremony on 27 August. The new decoration, the *Croix de guerre légionnaire*, had just been awarded for the first time after the German military authorities had been harassed about their wish to limit the Legion's first anniversary celebrations.

The legionnaires parade past General Galy, the Commissioner General of the Legion, on the Esplanade des Invalides.

The parade of volunteers pass the Chamber of Deputies as they return to their barracks after the ceremony.

Shortly before 5pm on 27 August, a detachment from the Tricolour Regiment, led by Colonel Puaud, head to the Arc de Triomphe to lay a wreath on the Tomb of the Unknown Soldier.

Colonel Puaud lays three wreaths on the Tomb of the Unknown Soldier. The wreaths were donated by the government, the Central Committee and the volunteers from the Legion.

The officers of the Tricolour Regiment in Guéret. Some of them would continue to go on and fight with the LVF, the French Militia or the Waffen SS.

Men of the 3rd Reinforcement Group in the Queen's barracks courtyard in Versailles. The photograph was taken on 8 October 1942, the day they left for three months' training at Kruszyna. On 7 January 1943, 109 of these men would be transferred to 3rd Battalion, whilst the rest of the Tricolour Regiment spent its last months in France.

II° anniversaire de la légion des Volontaires Français.27 Août 1943.
Défilé des légionnaires du front de l'Est sur l'Avenue des
Champs.-Elysées.-FU.

DEUXIEME ANNIVERSAIRE DE LA LEGION DES VOLONTAIRES FRANCAIS.
27 AOUT 1943.-APRES LA CEREMONIE A L'ARC DE TRIOMPHE, LE DRAPEAU
DE LA LEGION ET SA GARDE D'HONNEUR REGAGNENT LEUR CANTONNEMENT.
PHOTO SAF II44-20

Two postcards showing the parade down the Champs-Elysées on 27 August 1943, the second anniversary of the LVF's creation. Note the two Tricolour Regiment stamps issued the previous year by the post office. After the war the artist who designed these particular stamps, Gandon, was punished for having been seen as collaborating with the Vichy regime.

A postcard for the anti-Bolshevik exhibition, which comprised of photographs, posters as well as other visual propaganda and was held in various cities around France. One of the Tricolour Regiment stamps can be seen on the card, along with a postmark dated 4 May 1943 in Lyon.

Chapter Three

The African Phalanx

Created out of the ashes of the Tricolour Regiment, the *Französische Freiwilligen Legion,* more commonly known as the *Phalange africaine* (African Phalanx), was a unit of volunteers sent to fight in Tunisia, which at the time was still a part of the French Empire.

It all began on 8 November 1942 when Anglo-American troops landed on the coasts of Morocco and Algeria, in North Africa. Faced with this invasion, those French units loyal to Marshal Pétain fought for three days before signing an armistice on 10 November. The Minister of State, Admiral Platon, was sent on a mission to Tunisia to give government aid to the resistance, but this did not prevent the French Army in Africa from joining the Allies' side on 15 November. Despite the armistice agreement of 1940, the Axis powers failed to inform the Vichy government that it was sending German and Italian troops to occupy northern Tunisia. As a result, the head of the French government, Pierre Laval, decided to create a voluntary force to reclaim this area, and which soon became known as the African Phalanx. The Tricolour Regiment's recruitment offices were soon filled with eager men offering to join the fight. However, according to the Wehrmacht, problems with transporting the troops across the Mediterranean meant that when the troops finally arrived, they were no longer required. The German high command finally authorised the creation of an on-site fighting unit and six officers were flown to Tunis on 28 December 1942 to begin local recruitment.

The African Phalanx, known to the Germans as the *Kompanie Frankonia,* was symbolically integrated into the German Army in January 1943. It was attached to the 3rd Battalion of the 754th Panzergrenadier Regiment in the 334th Infantry Division of General Jürgen von Arnim's 5th Army. The Forgemol barracks served as the garrison while the Faidherbe barracks served as the depot. Both barracks were located in Tunis, along with the recruitment office, which opened on 1 January 1943. On 2 February a meagre company comprised of a number of Tunisians, departed for a two month training camp at Cedria-Plage, around 17km from Tunis. The Tunisians would later be removed from the company by the German authorities, who wanted to have closer control over them in other units. The recruits consisted of settlers, nationalist militants, students, NCOs and 'free' career soldiers.

The Phalanx was officially integrated into the 334th Division on 2 April 1943. After observing the French unit during combat exercises, the German Divisional Commander, Generalmajor Friedrich Weber, decided it was time for them to head for the Front. Dressed in German Infantry uniform, complete with German helmet and a blue, white and red rosette, the volunteers set off for their area of operations near the village of Medjez el-Bab, on the night of 8-9 April, where they relieved a German combat unit. Facing the five French sections, with a sixth remaining in camp to instruct the new arrivals, was the 78th Infantry Division of the British 1st Army. Their baptism of fire came on 14 April when the sector was heavily bombarded for two hours. On the night of 16-17 April an eight-man advance patrol was attacked by a detachment of fifty New Zealanders and Hindus. The French captured three prisoners as well as important documents. This action resulted in the 334th Division receiving its first citation and Generalmajor Weber was given three Iron Crosses to hand out in honour of the Führer's birthday.

On the night of 22 April the English guns pounded the phalanx's position, followed by an attack from the rear. American heavy tanks supported the English offensive and also attacked the Infantry. German smoke mortars then joined in and managed to stop the Anglo–American advance. The company and its many wounded retreated to its support positions and after twelve hours of fighting there were sixty missing soldiers, either dead or taken prisoner. The company was put into reserve on 25 April and under bombardment from the Allied forces, it retreated even further north over the following days before gathering on 6 May at the Faidherbe barracks in Tunis, with a fighting force of only sixty men. During the night, the company was disbanded on German orders. Due to a lack of resources, they were unable to withdraw to Italy and the Archbishop of Carthage granted protection to the soldiers and their families. When the Germans retreated, a small group of officers were evacuated to Italy by air. Back in Tunisia, those who had not been repatriated or had not managed to escape, were arrested by the French military. Some of these men were shot whilst others were integrated into French combat units and would later fight in France and Italy. A few months later, others members of the company were sentenced by the court in Algiers to varying degrees of punishment (death sentences as well as penal life sentences), including those who had been captured by the British.

18 March 1943, Camp Bordj-Cedria, Tunisia, where a formation of volunteers is being sworn in. A company of German paratroopers can be seen watching the event, while Colonel Kleber, surrounded by various members of the German authorities, attends as the OKW (Wehrmacht High Command) representative. German instructors, all with Russian combat experience, were sent to oversee the training of their future comrades and sessions had already been carried out with this parachute company, commanded by Lieutenant Von Bulow.

The French Resident-General in Tunisia, Admiral Estéva, congratulates two officers wearing the insignia of the unit: Commander Henri Curnier and Captain Daniel Peltier. This photograph, taken at the end of March 1943, also shows SS-Sturmbannführer Carlthéo Zeitschel (centre, back of image) and Lieutenant Charbonneau, a member of the Military Mission and the Phalanx's former propagandist on Vichy radio. The company's standard, adorned with the unit's insignia (the axe of Marshal Pétain), was blessed by a chaplain during an open-air ceremony, three days later.

Officers of the Tricolour Regiment at Guéret, Autumn 1942. It is from this regiment that the Germans authorised a military detachment in Tunisia, which would recruit contingents of both French and local men to fight the enemies of France and the Axis. Captain Henri Curnier is in the top-left of the photograph, with Commander Pierre Cristofini in bottom-right. Cristofini was flown to Tunisia on 28 December and on the same day was promoted to Lieutenant Colonel and head of the military detachment. Henri Curnier was promoted to Commander and worked as Cristofini's adjutant, as well as being his chief liaison with the German troops.

On 9 May 1943 Colonel Edgard
Puaud, Commander Henri
Curnier, wearing the insignia of
the Phalanx on his chest, and a
detachment from the LVF, laid
a wreath in Paris in memory of
the French who had died for the
defence of Tunisia. After having
been administratively attached
to the LVF on 5 May 1943, a
new law enacted on 19 May fully
integrated the African Phalanx
into the LVF. This meant that
its former members and their
families now had the same rights
as their peers on the Eastern
Front.

Legionnaire Jean Olmo, who lost both legs to frostbite whilst fighting on the Eastern Front, is decorated here by Commander Curnier on 10 May whilst at the convalescent home for severely injured LVF soldiers.

Commander Curnier arriving at the Hôtel de la Paix in Vichy, accompanied by Monsieur Bonnefoy, the Secretary-General for Information, about to present his experiences with the African Phalanx. The Germans awarded the Iron Cross to sixteen of its members.

After two stops in Italy the day before, at Naples and Turin, the last members of the French Military Mission arrive in Lyon on 14 May 1943, from Tunisia.

Now back home in France, Admiral Estéva welcomes the Phalanx officers who have come to greet him. In recognition of their patriotism they would be awarded the *Légion d'honneur* and *Croix de guerre légionnaire* in Vichy on 31 May, in the presence of President Pierre Laval and Captain Dupuis, who was awarded the *ordre de la Nation*. The officers would continue their adventures in either the LVF, the French Militia or the Waffen SS. (DR)

Pierre Lacomme, the provincial head of the SOL (*Service d'Ordre Légionnaire*) in Tunisia whose many members served in the Phalanx. He received the *Croix de guerre légionnaire* with bar in Vichy on 31 May, and became Inspector General of the French Militia after his return to metropolitan France.

The cover of the French edition of the German propaganda magazine, *Signal*, from 16 August 1943. It shows Captain André Dupuis, decorated on 29 April with the Iron Cross 2nd Class in Tunisia. The shot used here was taken on 31 May at the war memorial in Vichy, during the ceremony commemorating those who had fallen defending Tunisia, where he had also received the *Croix de guerre légionnaire.* This French decoration had been given to LVF members since 1942 and so by extension, was now awarded to members of the African Phalanx as well.

This is the number one propaganda journal for the French volunteers and shows General Bridoux, whose son served in the LVF, awarding Captain André Dupuis with his *Croix de guerre légionnaire* in Vichy on 31 May 1943.

Legionnaire Jacques Foratier in February 1944 at Camp Deba, in occupied Poland. He served with the African Phalanx in all its operations before flying from Tunis on 7 May 1943, surrounded by the British and Americans. His plane went down in flames over Sicily and he was hospitalised in Aversa. He returned to service on 17 July 1943 as a private 2nd class in the LVF and was sent to the Eastern Front at the end of the year. He was transferred to the Charlemagne Division in 1944 and ended the war as an Unterscharführer.

Chapter Four

The NSKK-Motorgruppe Luftwaffe

After the success of Operation Barbarossa, the Luftwaffe now needed drivers and mechanics to cover the losses it had suffered and to make sure that all lines of communication were working effectively, especially as they had now been stretched even further. In late July 1942, the first units of the Luftwaffe NSKK [a logistics corps of the Luftwaffe] were formed, which included French volunteers. Its main task was to ensure that supplies of food, fuel and ammunition reached the German Air Force in the occupied territories and especially immediately behind the frontlines.

The first 150 volunteers left Paris on 21 July 1942 and headed for the Vilvoorde barracks (a Brussels suburb), in Belgium, where the distribution centre for the NSKK was based. They were assigned to the 4th Regiment NSKK (which also included Dutch and Walloons) and began five months of basic training. Their instructors were former members of the German Army who were retired or released from service. With the arrival of fifty to sixty new volunteers each week, two transport companies were established in December 1942 and the 1st and 2nd companies of the 6th Battalion were stationed at the Schaffen Airfield and in Diest, respectively. First Company left for Stalino [Donetsk], Russia, in January 1943 and were assigned to the Rostov-on-Don region, close to the front. Second Company left for Kharkov in late February/early March 1943. Of the 124 trucks that set off, only 70 arrived in Kharkov, the rest having been left on the side of the road by order of the company commander and chief engineer. They wanted to return to Brussels and a peaceful life as quickly as possible, and so thought that the fewer vehicles they arrived with, the sooner they could head back. At the beginning of April, both companies, around 600 men in total, were back in Diest. The head of 2nd Company, keen to protect his own neck, wrote a report to the General Staff in Berlin accusing the French of incompetence, mismanagement and sabotage, and blamed them for the high number of abandoned vehicles. More than half of the workforce refused to sign a new contract of employment and were discharged soon after. Thirty French deserters from the NSKK presented themselves to the Waffen SS Ersatzkommando in Antwerp. They wanted to take a more active role in the fighting and to see more of their fellow compatriots incorporated into the Waffen SS. In the mean time, two other companies were formed in order to provide transportation for V1 rocket parts in northern France and to control the traffic around the launch sites.

With the last volunteers enrolled, the companies were consolidated and renamed, whilst 4th, 5th and 6th were integrated into the 2nd Battalion, 4th Regiment. These three companies were sent to a small Belgian town called Grammont to complete their basic military training, under the command of NSKK-Staffelführer, Josef Seigel, who would lead them until the end of the war. In late November the Wehrmacht sent the three companies to Brescia, Italy. The companies separated and left Brescia in early 1944, equipped with French and Italian vehicles of various sizes that they had been given when they arrived. From now on they were divided into a 'column', and each would live in its own quarters and work under its own administration. The 'columns' were scattered amongst the Italian civilian population, which for the most part accepted the volunteers, often allowing them to stay in their own homes. In return, as road signs and other infrastructure were disrupted and the railway stations bombed, the volunteers would sometimes take civilians in their trucks to other towns, in spite of the surveillance from the *Feldgendarmerie*. For two months they supplied the airports around Cassino with oil and gas, then carried bombs the 15km to Monte Cassino before heading to Florence and then down to Rome. These ammunition transports were carried out at night and had to be done without the use of headlights. Rules regarding safety were strict in terms of distances travelled, camouflage, routes taken and of course the schedules. The cabs of the large lorries became their home, where they would eat and sleep, and the drivers often lost their nerve as they were so tired from trying to escape from the attacking American aircraft. Contacts were established and relationships formed, but some did desert. The companies did not carry out these missions on behalf of the NSKK, but for the Luftwaffe. They also had to go out and look for trucks that had broken down on the roads so they could tow them back and repair them, as well as supply the batteries on Sardinia, which depended on the Luftwaffe. In August, whilst the Front in Bologna stabilised, there was an attempt to reconstruct the companies. However, supplies and equipment made it impossible; in one company, out of 300 men and 120 trucks at the beginning, there were now only 100 men and just 3 trucks.

In December 1944, after having handed in their trucks, they left Italy and were transferred to Denmark. They were to provide security to the airfield at Alesøe, where Messerschmitt planes had been grounded due to lack of fuel. They also worked in the shipyards at Odense and studied new anti-tank weapons. The companies were disbanded and the men and NCOs were each divided into groups of 400 men, plus staff. In January, the *Staffelführer* informed the assembled Battalion that a large French unit was being created within the Waffen SS, but no transfers were made. In late February/early March 1945, the first group was sent to the Hungarian Front, on the northern shore of Lake Balaton, where it saw a great deal of fighting due to the rapid advance of the Red Army. The second group left Denmark for Lake Balaton on 31 March, but withdrew when it reached Austria. The men were demobilised by NSKK-Hauptsturmführer, Hans Ströhle, on 29 April. Some decided to return to Italy, and a minority returned to their 'former landlords', where they had been happily housed, the year before.

This chapter ends with one final word on the Speer Legion, a subsection of non-Germans who served in the *NSKK-Transportbrigade*, but were not eligible for NSKK membership. Attached to the *OT-Einsatzgruppe West* in September 1943, it operated in five countries, each with a driving school and a mechanic. The West Speer Legion in Paris included Estonians, Ukrainians, French, Latvians, Lithuanians and Russians. Initial training took place near Paris, at Enghien-les-Bains, and included weapons handling, theoretical instruction on engines and car mechanics, before it moved to Nikolassee (in Berlin), at the Legion's education centre for motorised vehicles. The men wore a black uniform with an army belt, along with a police cap with an NSKK cockade on it, but were not allowed to carry weapons. They were employed by the Germans as drivers along the Atlantic coast, as well as being tasked to move vehicles between Germany, the General Government and various regions in the USSR, including anywhere from the Baltic to the Black Sea.

A photograph of 1st Company taken in January 1943 during a break from the frontlines. The road was in good condition as far as Lviv, in an acceptable condition from Lviv to Kovel (on the Russian border), but there was no road from Kovel to Kharkiv, so when all went well they could do 100km in 24 hours. In December 1942 an advance party made up of twenty-four Frenchmen and a German lieutenant had come to prepare the cantonments. (DR)

The local population cared little for politics and for centuries their land had regularly changed hands from one master to another. The volunteers slept in huts along with the chickens, lice and fleas. At the arrival of the 'liberators', the farmers were obliged to surrender the marital bed to the soldiers, although sometimes they wanted more than just the bed. (DR)

The Kharkiv region in the Ukraine in early 1943, in front of a destroyed Soviet road convoy. The free spare parts were a welcome sight for the mechanics. The journey was a real hassle for both the vehicles and the drivers: the drivers were out of practice, the engines were worn, the roads were rutted and the temperature was –28 degrees. (DR)

This image was also taken in the Kharkiv region, in front of another example of the remains that littered the roads. In Kharkiv itself, which had been taken by the Russians and then re-taken by the Germans, it was corpses that littered the deserted streets. Having your hands in your pockets was allowed as they were in a frontline zone. First Company spent two months between Donetsk and Dnipropetrovsk before returning, along with 2nd Company, after having had quite a few adventures, such as being surrounded and attacked by partisans. Around fifty volunteers were now missing. (DR)

Vandalised German graves around Kharkiv. In early 1943 2nd Company were quartered in Osnowa (a south-eastern suburb of Kharkiv). Over a fortnight, a section of the company transported 200 litres of gasoline from the railway station to the airfield, which works out at around 600 tonnes of fuel per day. They also carried bombs the 10km from the station to the airfield, where the Stuka bombers were waiting for them. They would fly out for a few kilometres, release the bombs and then return. There were plenty of planes, it was just the bombs

that were in short supply. However, two years later it would be the other way around as maintaining the aircrafts was virtually impossible. At the end of the month they suddenly received the order to return to Belgium. They were to leave the materials for the Germans who were to come and replace them. (DR)

NSKK-Untersturmführer André Györ (in the peaked cap), formerly of the Foreign Legion, is seen here behind the frontlines in Russia. He would later become an NSKK-Sturmführer and fought at Monte Cassino the following year. He disappeared in Hungary in 1945. (DR)

New volunteers arriving in Belgium at the end of February, 1943. They are wearing the Luftwaffe uniform, but the French among them are wearing a cloth badge on their left arm showing their three national colours (red, white and blue), superimposed with an axe (with a two-sided blade). At the top of the shield were the letters NSKK. Around their necks they also carried an oval metal ID tag, with the inscription MOT-GR-L-Ausl KRFTF. MOT for motor, GR for gruppe (group), L for Luftwaffe, Ausl for Auslander (foreigner) and KRFTF for Kraftfahrer (heavy goods vehicle driver). (DR)

Three NSKK-Oberscharführer in training at Geraardsbergen, Belgium, with Marz (from Alsace) on the left and Rupp in the middle. The latter would command the 3rd Column and ask to be transferred to the Wehrmacht in the summer of 1943, before leaving in July. Some men were sent to Stockel to become medics, to the driving school at Forest to gain their heavy goods vehicle licence, or to Tübingen, where the NSDAP had their driving school. The NSKK was originally a political party and so they would go there for a two month training period of theory lessons, videos and extensive practice. (DR)

Men of 3rd Column, 4th Company, in spring 1943 at the instruction school in Geraardsbergen, Belgium. From March to November they would travel across the plains of Belgium with packs on their backs, looking like well-off rag pickers. Lessons with machine guns, sub-machine guns, arm to arm combat, theory lessons, orienteering exercises; nothing was missed out. They spent more than six months on foot learning how to fire not only a Mauser, but also how to throw a grenade and dig fox holes. They needed to be occupied as there weren't actually any trucks for them. Often they went to the station to help the Red Cross nurses hand out dishes of rice. They could buy tobacco and beer on account and paid washerwomen to clean their laundry, as few washed their own. Some payments were made in kind, as the Flemish were not particularly rebellious. (DR)

Men of 3rd Column, 4th Company relaxing at Geraardsbergen in Spring 1943. Standing on the left are NSKK-Oberscharführer Marz and Rupp (without cap). In the foreground are two NCOs resting their heads together. The man in the hat with the eagle on his left arm is volunteer Puschmann, whose two step-sons died on 1 December 1941 whilst fighting with the LVF on the Russian Front. He joined the German motorised corps in order to get revenge. Later, a promotion by the Todt Organisation was called 'the Puschammn brothers promotion'. (DR)

The changing of the guard at Geraardsbergen, with Chamois from 4th Company, at the centre. (DR)

A room inspection of 4th Column. The main emblem of 4th Company, a panther, can be seen on the lockers. (DR)

A review of 2nd Battalion at Geraardsbergen in Autumn 1943 by the head of the NSKK, NSKK-Obergruppenführer von Bayer-Ehrenberg (centre), with NSKK-Staffelführer Josef Seigel on his left and Hans Ströhle on his right. The leaders had finally realised that drivers cannot be made from just words, and that military theory and endurance cannot be learned from songs. As a result, future drivers would undertake their training in Germany. (DR)

The first fabric badge sewn by the volunteers onto their left sleeve. In 1943 the name of the unit changed to *N.S.K.K. Transport Brigade der Luftwaffe* and so the fabric badge also changed, only retaining the three colours and the word France, written above. A horizontal bar was also sometimes sewn underneath the badge, signifying one year's combat service with the unit. (Coll. B. Destampes)

French trucks travel through the French village of Crécy-le-Ponthieu in Autumn 1943, transporting materials for the construction of the V1 launch site. Behind NSKK-Obergruppenführer von Bayer-Ehrenbeg, André S can clearly be seen with the shield on his arm. He would later become NSKK-Hauptscharführer, then NSKK-Truppführer and finally NSKK-Sturmführer. As Kolonführer of 4th Column, 4th Company, he was one of the few French column leaders and had a former soldier as his adjutant. They were both arrested in 1944 for various malpractices and handed over to the War Council at Parona airfield, near Verona. (DR)

Following the dismissal of Benito Mussolini by the Great Council of Fascism and the signing of the armistice between Marshal Badoglio and the Allies, a new theatre of operation opened up for the German Army. On their arrival in the new Italian Social Republic, the French took over the unoccupied Maggiore Giovanni Randaccio barracks in Brescia, Lombardy. The barracks formerly belonged to the 77th Regiment of the 7th Infantry Division 'Lupi di Toscana', which had been transferred to Rome in early September 1943. In the barrack courtyard, just before a big parade, NSKK-Oberscharführer Messer stands with NSKK- Truppführer Soyer on his right and NSKK-Rottenführer André Henriot sur on his left. As well as his tricolour badge, on his left sleeve can also be seen the driver's licence badge, which the men had to obtain if they wanted to drive. (DR)

A parade through the streets of Brescia in early 1944. The men were now paid in the Italian currency and were paid 150 *lire* every ten days. (DR)

Greeted here by fascists, the French head towards the Piazza del Duomo. (DR)

The people of Brescia watch a column as it takes part in a ceremonial parade, before the entire battalion regroups in front of the post office. (DR)

As the full force of the battalion joins together in Brescia, NSKK-Staffelführer Josef Seigel leads his men, with NSKK-Haupsturmführer Voll on his left (in the helmet). As commander of the 1st column he was a strict boss, but he was also full of humour and understanding. (DR)

L to R: Berthet, now NSKK-Scharführer; Henriot and NSKK-Sturmführer Leisner, at Pietola in Spring 1944. Henriot's epaulettes are braided in black, blue and silver. On his other side he wears the eagle, although it is not visible here. At this time, a great deal of gasoline was needed for the aeroplanes and the men were making trips of 700–800km almost every day. They came under fire from British planes, despite the surveillance equipment that monitored the skies in the hope of detecting enemy aircraft. (DR)

A sky blue cap badge that matched those of the French.

André Henriot in front of the entrance to where 443 Column were stationed at Pietola, in March 1944. From December 1944 the battalion's insignia was changed to the Eiffel Tower, replacing the panther that had been used in Belgium. The emblem can be seen on both the front of the truck and on the gatepost, and could still be found here several years after the war. Henriot had a Luftwaffe driving licence, which was grey in colour and made up of two parts. (DR)

An NSKK-Obersturmmann (SDG) medic poses with his comrades in front of a truck belonging to 443 Column at Pietola. André Henriot is the only one not wearing a helmet. Each column had a driver (the Kolonneführer), a medic, a mechanic, an MUG, a motorcyclist, a quartermaster and a cook. They were made up of two sections of twenty men (ten drivers and ten transporters, including a mechanic) each. (DR)

The volunteers from 443 Column during a stop on the road by the side of the River Po, in early summer, 1944. The NSKK-Scharführer (second from right) can be seen holding a signal. During a march, a five minute break was scheduled every hour so that the stragglers could catch up. If a vehicle broke down in front of him, each driver had to maintain the space in the line so that they could get back into position during one of these breaks - provided that it was only a minor problem. Note that the volunteers had to drive in broad daylight, despite the threat of being attacked by enemy aircraft, whilst the Germans travelled at night in order to avoid being attacked. (DR)

Hans Ströhle, Kompanieführer of 4th Company, wearing his tropical uniform, which only a few men had in Summer 1944, seen here during a decoration ceremony. In June fifteen *Croix de fer* and *Croix du mérite* were handed out for action in Italy. As well as these awards, driver's medals and promotions were also given. (DR)

NSKK-Obertsturmführer Hans Ströhle at San Martino Buon Albergo in Summer 1944. Almost all of the material had been burned and destroyed by the fighter planes. The main roads had also been damaged and so only a few small journeys were possible. (DR)

French volunteers at the fuel depot near Ferrara, not far from where 443 Column was stationed. After the attack against Hitler on 20 July, their ID card was amended and they were no longer to be treated as non-combatants. Later, some would see action in Piedmont, fighting against the increasingly aggressive Communist partisans. (DR)

The 5th Company of French Volunteers at a railway station. Staebler, a medic, can be seen in the front row on the left, wearing an armband. Jean-Pierre B is in the centre with his hands clasped together. They were both among the first to sign up in July 1942. (DR)

A morning stop and musical break at the main train station in Augsburg on their way to Denmark, December 1944. Second from the left is NSKK-Scharführer Camille S., the mechanic for 5th Column, 4th Battalion, and a former engineer in the French Navy. (DR)

Grenzübertrittschein West Nr. 24 863

Der Kraftfahrer
(Dienstgrad — Dienstbezeichnung — Beruf)

Robert S

(Vor- und Zuname)

Dienststelle Legion Speer, Berlin Feldpost-Nr.:

ist berechtigt, die Grenze...... zwischen — dem Reich
Frankreich

und Belgien — Frankreich .... unter Vorlage
des Dienstausweises

Nr. 66 53

in der Zeit
vom 12.Mai 194 4 bis zum 3. Juni 194 4

an den zugelassenen Übergangsstellen
einmal¹) und zurück¹) —   wiederholn);
zu überschreiten.

   Beim letzten Grenzübertritt ist der Schein an der Über-
gangsstelle abzugeben.

                              Den 12. Mai 194 4

                              Der Generalquartiermeister
(Stempel)   I. A.

                              (Unterschrift)

¹) Nichtzutreffendes streichen   Hauptmann

Document belonging to volunteer Robert S. from the Speer Legion, showing the dates given for his leave; 12 May–3 June 1944.

Chapter Five

The Todt Organisation

Headed by Oberbaudirecktor Karl Weis, chief engineer with the *Militärbefehlshaber West*, the *Todt Organisation Einsatzgruppe West* had been stationed in Lorient, Brittany, since May 1940. As agreed with the military services and the central Todt Organisation in Berlin, its main priority was the building of the Atlantic Wall in 1942, before heading south to build the coastal defences along the Mediterranean. On the construction sites, French workers were required to mix with their compatriots who had been forced to remain in the country playing the black market and other lucrative deals and thus avoiding compulsory work service in a factory in Germany. They were completely dependent on the *Französische Frontführung* [French Front Guide], a French department based in Paris and led by *Haupttruppführer* Camille Sinniger, a former member of the LVF, who had been given the highest military rank granted to a foreigner. In addition to the many forced labourers there were around 5,000 Frenchmen in uniform, who volunteered for the service. This led to the subsequent departure of many members of the Todt Organisation (TO), who wished to join units that were more active in combat.

There were militarised workers (*Frontarbeiter*) present in all of the Wehrmacht's theatres of operation. They built bridges, modified fortifications, built roads, and oversaw the delivery of fuel and supplies. Until November 1942, members of the TO were regarded as *Wehrmachtsgefolge* [Wehrmacht followers], and remained independent of the army they were accompanying. This status was shown on their identity tags and pay books in order to avoid possible sanctions should they be arrested as snipers. After November 1942 they were issued with an army booklet labelled *WH Festungsbau* [*Wehrmacht Heer Festungsbau* - German Army Fortress Builder], and were included in the regular armed forces. They wore a swastika armband on their left sleeve and sometimes carried a weapon, depending on their location and availability in Europe or Russia, to counter possible attacks from partisans that sometimes resulted in injury or death. As a result, the TO decided to carry weapons in order to defend itself in various locations and set up its own protection units.

These armed detachments were drawn from the workers themselves and were called *Schutzkommandos*. They had their own ranks, which were gradually filled with volunteers of various nationalities, including French. They were equipped with a variety of small arms with the objective of maintaining order in the free workers' camps on the construction sites, as well as guarding strategic buildings and facilities. After an internship that would normally last for one month, or longer if necessary, the French groups were assigned to various ports along the English Channel and the Atlantic coast. Over time it is possible to see where the German Army was present (Latvia, Norway etc.). In the summer of 1943, all existing TO *Schutzkommandos* composing of up to ten battalions were distributed according to the Army Groups. Those of the *Einsatzgruppe West* became the 11th Battalion and were divided into ten sections and groups. It withdrew to Germany in August 1944.

Ahead of the increase in the number of workers on its sites, the TO was concerned about the well-being of its employees. In November 1942 it created a team of 'social inspectors', whose recruitment was entrusted to Camille Sinniger. He primarily chose former members of the reformed LVF, who still wanted to serve according to the original ideals they had had when they first volunteered. In the TO camps throughout France, their presence made them a buffer between the Germans and the workers who might not have had the same mentality, or the same discipline. They were responsible for the welfare of the civilians and acted as advisers and liaison between the workers, the building companies, the German authorities and the French services, for everything related to social issues and the basic material requirements for life. Their training took place at a school in Brittany, under the direction of French teachers and instructors. For a period of around three weeks their schedule was devoted to physical exercises, courses in hygiene and how to solve social problems that might arise regularly in a camp, as well as how to combat hostile propaganda.

There were also transmission teams and telephone operators who were trained in France and at the Barten camp in East Prussia. The latter closed in November 1943 and training continued in France from the beginning of 1944, with training programmes of two months at Camp Beauregard, which also housed the *Schutzkommandos*. The paid training was designed to help the volunteers work with experienced engineers fitting telephone lines. One team was en route to Russia when Pietro Badoglio, the head of the Italian Government, announced the armistice between the Italians and the Allies. As the Italians abandoned the fighting, the team was sent to Yugoslavia to relieve them. Here the French were constantly beaten by the armies of Tito in the defensive positions assigned to them, and because the difficult conditions were not suited for combat.

There was also a unit called *NSKK Transportgruppe Todt*, whose staff were under the control of the NSKK. The French in their khaki uniforms with short jackets, like those of the German Army, served as military vehicle drivers on behalf of the TO, but were different from those of the *NSKK Motorgruppe Luftwaffe*, who wore a grey-blue uniform and worked for the German Air Force, distinguishing themselves on the Russian and Italian Fronts. Finally, the TO also employed women in different French camps. In addition to those who worked as typists and interpreters, there were also several hundred who served in uniform, mainly as nurses. As in most German organisations that accepted foreign nationals, these French auxiliary women wore a badge on their national uniform.

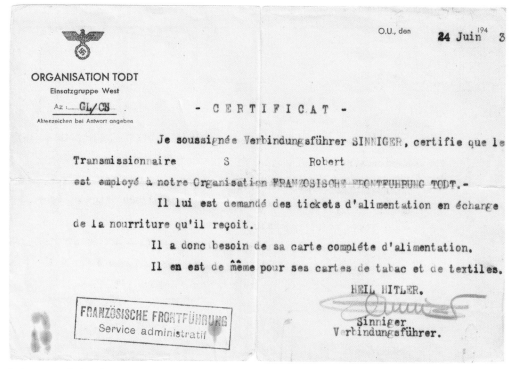

A document belonging to Robert S. of *OT Einsatzgruppe West*, dated 24 June 1943 and signed by Camille Sinniger. Robert S. enlisted in Paris on 15 March 1943 and was sent to a training school in Ponthierry, under the command of OT-Frontführer Peters, a German. There were around seventy French volunteers there, as well as more elderly Germans and they learnt the basic theories of electricity, maintaining a field telephone and how to set up a line. After three weeks of training and having taken the loyalty oath, he was appointed as a telephone engineer in Paris, where he used an automated telephone, not a field one. He found himself in a team of specialised civilian workers who had to install and maintain the telephone network in Paris for the Todt Organisation and NSKK. He had his own service book and uniform with its specialist insignia and was often mistaken for a German by the local populace, who did not always see the tricolour badge on his arm. In May 1944 he requested to be released from the Todt Organisation and joined the Kriegsmarine as a *Matrose* (sailor). (Coll. R.S.)

The former legionnaire Camille Sinniger, the head of the *Frontführung der Französischen Unterführer Korps* and Todt Organisation Social Inspectors, seen here in Spring 1942. He was among the first fifty volunteers to enlist with the LVF, eventually gaining the rank of lieutenant. Here he is wearing the *Winterschlacht im Osten 41/42* ribbon, along with the insignia of his former unit, the LVF, on his arm. He was killed during a *Maquis* attack in France on 19 July 1944, after having joined the French Militia. (DR)

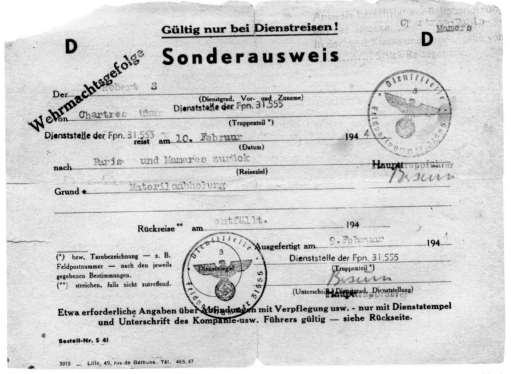

A special permit from February 1944 allowing OT-Mann Robert S. to travel to the location specified. (Coll. R.S.)

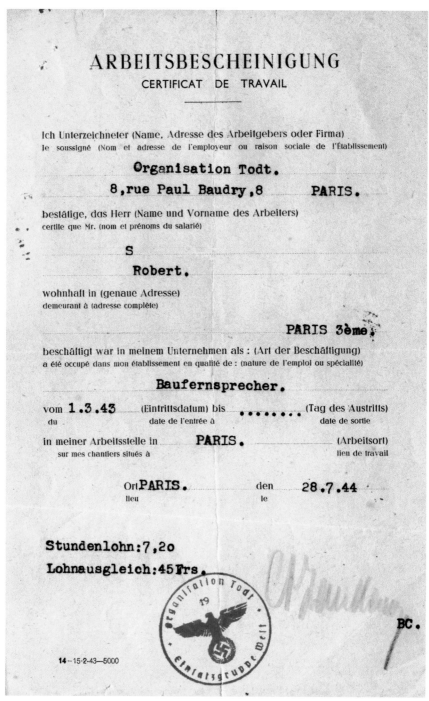

A work certificate for telephone engineer (Baufernsprecher) Robert S., due to expire at the end of July 1944, stating that he worked for the Todt Organisation. He had actually been enlisted in the Kriegsmarine since May of that year. (Coll. R.S.)

OT-Schutzkommandos at the Beauregard training camp (Ausbildungslager - Lehrgang West) at La Celle-Saint-Cloud, near Paris, in 1943. Military training was no longer carried out in Brittany, but in the former French camp for German prisoners. The *OT-Einsatzgruppenstab* (Operational HQ) had been transferred to Paris on 9 April 1943.

During their training, the Schutzkommandos wore caps, as well as a swastika armband on their left arm. (DR)

The future Todt Organisation camp supervisors during their training at Celle-Saint-Cloud. (DR)

An inspection by the head of the *OT-Zentrale*, Oberministerialrat Xaver Dorsch, who walks past the men, accompanied by Braun, the head of the *OT-Lehrlangers West*. In the Paris region, the men were spread out over various construction sites, airfields and underground factories. (DR)

Camp Beauregard had been refurbished and modernised and now had many new workshops and facilities. It also now had *Bewährer-Männer* (watchmen), whose job was to protect those factories that worked for the Todt Organisation. (DR)

A group of French guards from Einsatzgruppe 'West', seen here at Oberlauteintung Biskaya, in south-west France. In a turn towards a more paramilitary involvement, in March 1943 the men saw their service books withdrawn and were instead given a *Soldbuch*.

19 June 1943. A former member of the LVF who is now a social inspector, accompanies legionnaires marching through Paris wearing his black uniform. The social inspectors also wore a black tie, dark blue shirt and a silver braided hat with no obvious insignia. The rank insignia were those of the Todt Organisation. The 'Org. Todt' armband was sometimes worn at the bottom of the left arm, whilst the nationality badge was worn between the elbow and shoulder of the opposite arm. Decoration ribbons, whether French or not, could be worn on the chest. Some also wore the armband showing they were veterans of the Legion (red with a white circle and a golden eagle with a tricolour shield at the centre), which could be worn with or without the 'Org. Todt' armband. The outbreak of the Second World War had transformed this civilian organisation (composed of recruited workers, engineers and managerial staff employed by their firms) into a paramilitary unit, responsible for all strategic work where the interests of German troops were involved.

The LVF chaplain, Mayol de Lupé, seen here in his army uniform, gives a speech at the Salle Wagram, Paris, on 22 June 1943. To commemorate the second anniversary of German troops entering Russia, a delegation of four French OT nurses are being presented with an armband of their unit and a flag bearing a red cross, whilst flanked by legionnaires. They are wearing dark blue shirts with their nationality badge between the elbow and shoulder on their right arm. On their opposite arm they wear the armband bearing the inscription 'Org.Todt'. On their left chest pocket is a cloth badge showing a red cross in a white cog. The rest of their uniform comprises of a skirt, belt buckle and black tie. They too carry a *Dienstbuch* (logbook), which contains their contact information, blood group, serial number and activities.

In the second row are volunteers from the *Parti Franciste* (a fascist and anti-Semitic league) who have enlisted in the Todt Organisation and are seen here marching on the Champs-Elysées in Paris on 4 July 1943. The men on the front row are members of the LVF.

Before being killed by partisans in France in the summer of 1944 during the German Army's retreat, OT-Kriegsberichterstatter Flamand A. Kurvers took this photograph of the organisation's French orchestra. The seventeen volunteer workers are pictured here on 8 November 1943, rehearsing for a ceremony to be held the following day. The cloth badge of the organisation's French volunteers is worn on the right arm. It is a red cog, the emblem of the *Deutsche Arbeitsfront*, with a red white and blue shield and topped with the word France. (DR)

A delegation from the Todt Organisation, including a social inspector in the centre, photographed on 9 November 1943. They are commemorating the march on the 'Feldherrnhalle', by laying a wreath under the Arc de Triomphe, at the Tomb of the Unknown Soldier.

Dependant on the Todt Organisation and not the Wehrmacht, three of these volunteers are wearing an armband showing they are LVF veterans. They are commemorating the twentieth anniversary of the Munich Putsch in 1923.

Among the civilians and militiamen, a member of the Todt Organisation in the second row is preparing to leave for his new unit, the Waffen SS, along with this contingent who are gathered in Paris in October 1943. (DR)

Chapter Six

The Kriegsmarine

In 1941 Germany had conquered many nations bound by seas and oceans. Countless ports were fortified and put into operation to help with the fighting, as well as for use for the submarine service. The French worked as engineers, technicians and civilian workers in the national ports where the Germans now had bases. The time had not yet come for compulsory military service.

It wasn't until nearly three years after the hostilities began on the Eastern Front, on 17 March 1944, that legislation was enacted in France. The government finally allowed its countrymen to serve in the German Navy (Kriegsmarine) and gave them the same benefits under the laws and regulations of the LVF. Nevertheless, for a long time those who lived by the sea (in Normandy and Brittany) had already worked in the local offices (or in Germany with the free workers). Around 2000 French worked for the Kriegsmarine, but only on an individual basis.

There are two main factors that explain the delay in the recruitment process: from a prestige point of view, it was hard for the Germans to believe that a foreign volunteer might appear on the decks of one of its warships. They were only there to supplement personnel, not as an incorporated unit. Furthermore, there was a lengthy discussion between Dönitz and Himmler regarding European volunteers, resulting in a great deal of time lost for formal recruitment. The Reichsführer finally agreed, and assigned those individuals who possessed knowledge of the sea, or whose businesses were linked to the sea, on the condition that they received political training by the SS at the Sennheim training camp in Alsace.

In 1943 the 28th Naval Depot was also used by the Waffen SS (*28. Schiffsstammabteilung*). This depot was specifically responsible for the basic training of foreign volunteers and received recruits from Belgium, the Netherlands, Latvia, Ukraine, Spain, France and Denmark. Due to a shortage of officials, the German training staff changed over the months and officers became increasingly rare on smaller vessels and submarines. Upon their arrival, the French were sorted and grouped by section or company, with numbers varying from 250 to 450 men for a total of 11 companies. Some were made up exclusively of French, whilst others were mixed. After they were assigned they were handed their German uniform: navy blue, field grey and a general blue one for all occasions. The latter uniform was distributed and worn after they had sworn their oath, marking the end of their initial training, which usually lasted between six and eight weeks. They were then transferred to specialist schools in Germany, notably Mannheim, Duisburg or Varel. Then followed rifle training at 'soldier school', and training at 'sailor school' (manoeuvring a canoe on a river or lake) for about three months. They were then assigned to a naval unit, usually on smaller vessels (minesweepers, patrol boats etc.) and mainly on the Baltic, at Kiel. They were rarely sent to the Mediterranean or the North Sea, and only the very first Frenchmen who signed up in the four initial companies actually set sail and engaged in fighting at sea. After the attempted assassination of Hitler on 20 July 1944, Himmler changed his mind about French sailors. Whilst some remained at their posts with the support of their superiors, many of them unwittingly ended up joining the Waffen SS, after having been trained by them in the first place. The majority of them found themselves integrated into the newly formed SS Charlemagne Brigade, including two sailors who would later be awarded the *Ritterkreuz* (Knight's Cross) in 1945.

There were also compatriots who belonged to the *Kriegsmarinwerftpolizei* (Shipyard Police), a unit created in early 1943 on the initiative of the Kriegsmarine services based at La Pallice, on the Atlantic Coast. Within this Franco-German paramilitary group, the French consisted mostly of LVF veterans, who protected and monitored the German shipyards and submarine bases, armed with guns. These men are not to be confused with the *Kriegsmarine-Wehrftmänner* (Naval Shipyard Guards), another unit created in late 1941, with the similar aim of protecting the naval arsenals in Brittany, but who wore a different coloured uniform.

Identity card of a member of the *Kriegsmarinwerftpolizei*, who was employed to guard the German naval base at Saint-Nazaire in October 1943. *(Coll. J.P. Lamotte)*

Kriegsmarine auxiliaries can be seen in their dark uniform just behind a member of the LVF, at a meeting of the pro-German movement, the PPF [French Popular Party], in Paris on 8 August 1943. Frenchmen in the German Navy did not wear any distinctive emblems, unlike their compatriots in the Waffen SS or NSKK, who had a tricolour badge stitched onto their sleeve.

The complete staff of *Schiffstammabteilung 28* from 1 December 1943 to 31 March 1944. From left to right: Ensign 2nd Class (MA) Gowen; Ensign 1st Class (MA) Hoech, commander of 3rd Company; Ensign 1st Class (MA) Hah, commander of 5th Company; Lieutenant Commander (MA) Wellner, commander of 1st Company; Lieutenant Commander (MA) Dr Gobel, the *Schiffstammabteilung 28* doctor; Commander (MA) Dr. Schneider, commander of *Schiffstammabteilung 28*; Ensign 1st Class (MA) Dr. Bruckmann, commander of 4th Company; Ensign 2nd Class (MA) Kohler; Lieutenant (MA) Hoffmann , commander of 2nd Company; Ensign 2nd Class (MA) Esch; Ensign 2nd Class (MA) Wilhelm; Ensign 2nd Class (MA) Frischauf, the adjutant; Ensign 1st Class (MA) Benz, the administrative officer.

The Oath of Loyalty was a tradition in the German Army and until it was taken the volunteers were able to leave at any time. Only Hitler, as head of the Third Reich, could release a soldier from his oath. The day would arrive when the soldiers received their dark blue uniforms, which would be theirs until they left the service. After their weeks at the training camps, they were deemed fit to be members of the German Navy and to wear the uniform. Here the young French, Dutch and Flemish volunteers from Lieutenant Commander Weller's 1st Company make their oath at Sennheim in the first trimester of 1944. The band play the famous '*Wir fahren gegen Engeland*' (We Sail Against England), while the commander gave a short speech from a decorated podium. The men then lined up in front of a flag from a destroyer sunk off the coast of Narvik in 1940 and touched it with their hand, just like the 17-year-old boy from Brittany, on the right. They saluted with their other hand, folding all but the middle and index fingers, and swore the oath. After a rendition of '*Deutschland über alles*' and '*Horst Wessel Lieb*', played by the marine band, came a triple '*Sieg Heil*!', which marked the end of the ceremony and the start of a little free time for the sailors. (*Coll. R. S.*)

A photograph of the French volunteers taken in Spring 1944 during their transportation from Mannheim to Varel. Their conditions of enrolment meant that they enjoyed the same training and promotion available to their German comrades, as well as the same treatment, food and equipment. In addition, their families also benefited from various allowances. (*Coll. R. S.*)

A French group of volunteers receiving training at Varel in the spring of 1944, under the leadership of Maat Holzapfel. The 28th Naval Depot at Sennheim was subordinated to the 8th *Schiffstammregiment*, located at Varel, who commanded the North Sea. (*Coll. R. S.*)

A group of French volunteers from 6th Company, which was made-up entirely of French, in May–June 1944 at Sennheim. They had no contact with the Waffen SS at the camp, even if they sometimes shared their facilities. This company was sent to a specialist school in Duisburg and afterwards became 2nd Company. From here they were sent en masse to the Charlemagne Brigade in September, without being told in advance that this would happen. The brigade authorities tried to lure them there with the idea of becoming a *Sosstrupp* (attack troop), with ultra modern equipment and camouflage. Some of the men accepted this as a done deal, but most refused to abandon the uniform that they were so proud of. In the end, very few sailors were released from their commitments.

Chapter Seven

The Franzosische-SS-Freiwilligen-Sturmbrigade No.8

On 30 January 1943 Hitler signed the order for the creation of a French unit in the Waffen SS. The order was immediately relayed by Himmler's representative in France, SS-Brigadeführer Karl Oberg, the senior SS commander whose departments could now begin to make contact with those in the collaborationist circles, as well as those at the German Embassy in Paris. Although nearly 300 of their compatriots had already taken the plunge and were already serving in divisions such as the *5th SS Panzer Division Wiking* and the *3rd SS Panzer Division Totenkopf*, which included Walloons and Flemings born in northern France (which was then under German military administration), the majority of the French were waiting for the green light from Marshal Pétain's government.

A decree issued on 22 July 1943 declared that the French state authorised its citizens to join the Waffen SS, giving them the same benefits as those members of the LVF, which was seen as a serious rival to recruitment. A recruitment office (*Ersatzkommando Frankreich der Waffen SS*) was opened in Paris, although it was also possible to sign up at German police stations and at regional prefecture headquarters. Prisoners of War were allowed to join, as well as forced labourers working in Germany. Lodged in Paris, the new recruits were then sent to the Sennheim training camp in Alsace to begin their military training. To comply with this government legislation published in July, a new contract had to be signed by those who had joined up before this date. The average age of the French volunteers was very young, and just like others who had enlisted before them, they wanted to prove to their superiors that despite coming from a country that had been defeated in June 1940, they deserved their place in the Waffen SS. Future officers and leaders were chosen from the individuals who stood out. Those with NCO potential were sent to the *SS Unterführerschule* at Posen-Treskau, whilst officer candidates went to the *SS Junkerschule* at Bad Tölz. Other recruits went to different schools, depending on what they were to specialise in. Some were transferred to the specialist SS commando school at Hildesheim or were sent to recruit other civilian workers or PoWs. The French would also act as SS war correspondents and in other general units where their rank was deemed sufficient enough for an assignment.

In 1944 the majority of troops were sent to the Beneshau camp in the Protectorate of Bohemia and Moravia, in order to form an artillery regiment. Due to a lack of qualified French officers, the brigade was transformed into a *Sturmbrigade* (Assault Brigade) of two battalions and was officially hereafter called the *Franzosische-SS-Freiwilligen-Sturmbrigade Nr.8. (Franz. Nr.1)* and was commanded by *SS-Sturmbannführer* Paul-Marie Gamory-Dubourdeau.

After a trip to Networschitz, three infantry companies, one heavy equipment company and one Pak company were formed. The unit was cleansed of all those with criminal records and of those who had failed to report cases incompatible with the SS code of honour. These men were immediately kicked out and sent to concentration camps. The conditions at Networschitz were not conducive to training and the brigade moved once more, to Neweklau, near Prague. Training there was mainly centred around anti-tank combat, with the arrival of the Panzerfaüste and Panzerschreck weapons. Despite the difficulty of conducting both day and night exercises, which inevitably resulted in casualties, enthusiasm was high amongst the men, who believed that their departure to the Front was close. In late July, whilst 2nd Battalion continued its training in the former Polish corridor from Danzig to Schwarnegast, 1st Battalion was now combat ready and awaiting its departure orders.

A total of 980 men under the command of SS-Hauptsturmführer Pierre Cance landed in Galicia, Turkey, on 5 August, on what was then the Eastern Front. They were attached to the *18th SS-Freiwilligen-Panzer-Grenadier-Division Horst Wessel* and their mission was to reduce the salient and align the frontline along the railway line from Sanok to Krakow. Their first actions were carried out under the admiring eyes of Wehrmacht officers, with Horst Wessel mentioning the unit in his divisional dispatches. Holed up in the abandoned Russian positions, the French underwent several bombing raids up until Tuesday, 15 August. This was the last stage of the counter-offensive and after much fierce fighting and numerous fatalities, the French finally achieved their goal. As the Wehrmacht soldiers relived their positions, the *Sturmbrigade* fell back to Wolica, where officers estimated that they had around 130 dead or wounded.

After 24 hours, the revised units joined another sector of the frontline, where there were cracks everywhere. In Dębrica, Poland, they were spread over a 15km front along the Wisłoka River. On the morning of 20 August the Soviet artillery bombarded their positions and the battalion collapsed within hours. Scattered along their new defensive lines, on 22 August the French battalion, already depleted by the loss of so many soldiers and officers, attempted to defend the village of Mokré. Its commander, Cance, was wounded for a third time and the decision was taken to evacuate westwards. From those who had landed at the front in August, the rough casualty list shows that more than 100 men had died, 40 were prisoners or missing and more than 660 were wounded. Of the 15 officers, 7 were dead and 8 were missing. The units were reorganised around the survivors, commanded by SS-Obersturmführer Jean Croisile. Three companies were established, each with between forty and sixty men, including those who were hospitalised with minor injuries. On 24 August, 1st Battalion was cited in Horst Wessel's divisional order before it left Tarnów station, heading for Bruss in the Polish Corridor.

The first medical examination on 13 August 1943 in Paris with SS-Haupt. Otto Ebner. Germany was in desperate need of fresh blood, in order to continue fighting in what was now the fourth year of conflict. Any applicants who did not pass here were certainly passed on to other paramilitary units, whose acceptance levels were lower. Around 50 per cent of volunteers were eliminated in the first months following their medical examination and an interview regarding their motives for volunteering. They had to prove their membership of the Aryan race, have no criminal convictions and applicants for privates must be aged between seventeen and forty, which was a little higher than the French Army. (DR)

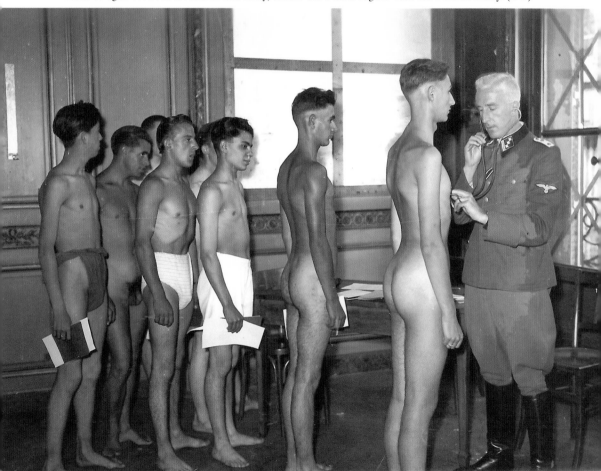

A propaganda postcard similar to a famous poster for French volunteers, but slightly modified here for members of the Walloon Legion.

The back of a propaganda booklet aimed at the French. The content was also published in other languages, although the images remained the same. The number of volunteers was lower than that expected to create a division as originally envisioned by the SS-Führungshauptamt (the operational command of the SS). The decision to form a regiment was eventually taken on 16 October 1943.

A contingent departs from Paris in 1943, heading for Sennheim (Cernay). Numerous inscriptions in chalk can be seen written on the cars. (DR)

A snapshot from October 1943 showing the enthusiasm that followed the Waffen SS being opened to the French. A high profile press conference was held in Paris on 6 August, announcing the formation of a French battalion (the precursor of the regiment that was to follow), and that it was a combination of both French and German officers. As always, propaganda meant that exaggerations were made about the actual number of soldiers enrolled at the time. (Coll. Bundesarchiv)

Originally reserved for 'German' volunteers before being opened up to western occupied countries in August 1943, Sennheim Camp was commanded by SS-Oberführer Fick, seen here on the left, then by SS-Oberführer Jacobsen. Facing him is Jean de M., who had joined up before his eighteenth birthday. After the *Sturmbrigade* he was transferred to the *Aufklärungszug* (reconnaissance sector) of the 57th Regiment, Charlemagne Division, and took part in the fighting in Pomerania. For a time there were more French in the camp than any other nationality, to the point that they soon had an entire company: 1st Company, 1st Battalion. This company was made up of the initial volunteers, with 2nd Company, created at the end of September, being made up of labourers and PoWs from the German Stalags. (DR)

Training at Sennheim was often conducted by injured veterans from Germany, Luxembourg, Flanders etc. and consisted mainly of intensive physical exercises, political and racial classes and basic military training that lasted for three months. The uniform and collar tabs (spiegels) were the same as all Waffen SS units. On the one side were the rank and distinction badges, whilst on the other were the two silver Ss on a black background. These were handed out without ceremony to each volunteer at Sennheim. To begin with, sportswear was generally worn, as seen in this photograph taken in October 1943 of Jean C., whose brothers would also enrol in the SS. On the left is Charles D., who had been at the camp since the 21st of the month. He would undertake his NCO training at Posen from 18 January 1944 and later be killed in Pomerania in 1945. On the right is Hervé L., who was also at the camp from 21 October 1943 until February 1944. He was made SS-Rottenführer in August and finished as SS-Oberscharführer in the 57th Regiment of the Charlemagne Division. (DR)

On January 4 1944, whilst the first French SS volunteers returned to Sennheim by train after their leave in order to continue their specialist training, the railway was sabotaged resulting in many casualties and fatalities as they entered the station. On 10 January another ten volunteers were killed after an ammunition wagon that was being unloaded at Sennheim station blew up, with another soldier dying the following day as a result of his injuries. SS-Schütze Andreas Terveer, a Dutchman, is seen here acting as sentinel to the coffins. The camp commander's wreath bears the words 'SS-Al Sennheim'. (DR)

New Waffen SS recruits from all over France are seen here swearing the oath in early 1944, at the *Ersatzkommando Frankreich* headquarters in Paris. Among them, on the left, is François Barazer, from Lannurien, whose son was a member of the Charlemagne Division that would end up fighting in Berlin in 1945. As with all units composed of foreign volunteers, including ethnic Germans, its name was always 'SS- Freiwilligen...' preceded by a number showing its creation date. On 8 October it took the name *8.Französische SS-Freiwilligen Grenadier Regiment*, before being changed on 12 November to the *Französische SS-Freiwilligen Regiment 57*, and finally became the *Französische SS-Freiwilligen Regiment 57 (Französische No.1)* in January 1944. (DR)

Volunteer Fernand Costabrava in Spring 1944 after he'd moved from the NSKK to the Waffen SS. At Sennheim he would have seen a form of natural selection taking place between those who resisted discipline, training, the marches and those who gave up morally and physically, not counting the 'undesirables' who left for various reasons. As such, the camp actually worked as a 'triage' centre. (DR)

The badge of the French flag that was worn on the left sleeve. (Coll. B.Destampes)

SS-Std.Ob.ju. Abel Chapy, a former officer in the French Army. Although he had no right to his former rank upon his arrival at Sennheim in 1943, he quickly reached the rank of SS-Oberschärführer. His training at the camp was identical to that given an NCO, so that he knew what his assistants were doing, how to follow commands in German and of course, sport and political instruction. Along with twenty-five other officers and midshipmen, on 6 January he was sent to a special training school at Bad Tölz in the Bavarian Alps. This first specialist training for French officer-cadets (conducted in groups and not individually, as before) lasted for nine weeks, from 10 January to 11 March 1944 and was intended to upgrade their training and their education in warfare methods used by the Waffen SS. Chapy distinguished himself during the fighting in Galicia and on his orders, at the end of August 1944, four individuals would challenge the German Quartermaster, Egl, for embezzlement and against the false report of desertion that had been registered. SS-Ustuf. Neubaeur filed a complaint with the police in Tarnow, leading to the arrest of Chapy and his accomplices. (DR)

A group of volunteers dressed in camouflage at Networschitz, around 50km from Prague and 10km from Benešov. Since the end of 1942, this village and its surrounding countryside had been emptied of its inhabitants and used for military training. This is where the soldiers finally encountered their French officers, who were fresh out of training. After a rather frosty first meeting with their compatriots, five companies were formed and work immediately resumed. Administrative documents from Alsace and Lorraine were mixed with the French, so as to better understand the language of Goethe. (DR)

French volunteers training with an MG 42 in the woods at Networschitz. It was extremely cold and the troops were housed in dilapidated or abandoned buildings. The brigade soon moved a further few kilometres to Neveklov, where a Walloon Battalion of the Waffen SS had left little behind. (DR)

The *Sturmbrigade* staff at Neweklau, photographed on 11 June 1944. L to R: Joseph Pleyber; Marcel Herpe; two French SS nurses; the doctor, SS-Ostuf. Pierre Bonnefoy; former militiaman, Paul P.-B.; nurse Paulette; SS-Ustuf. Jean Croisile; unit commander SS-Ostubaf. Paul-Marie Gamory-Dubourdeau and SS-Std.Ob.ju. Henri Kreis. (DR)

Having said goodbye to Sennheim, the troops headed for Prague on 13 January to continue their training. As they were transformed into SS-Kanonier, at the wish of the Reichsführer, their training also consisted of bringing guns to the battery, although they did not actually fire them. Those who were not tattooed at Sennheim were tattooed at the local hospital, where their female compatriots were also serving. These French women had joined the Waffen SS as German Red Cross nurses and had first trained at Spa in Belgium, then at a hospital (usually in Germany), before being deployed to the SS Podol hospital or Felzengrund in Prague, after their exams. One of these nurses can be seen here, recognisable by the eagle on her left arm and surrounded by her compatriots on the training ground at Neweklau, on 11 June 1944. (DR)

A photograph taken on the training ground at Neweklau, 11 June 1944. L to R: volunteer Henri Kreis; Joseph Pleyber; SS Sister Nelly, from the hospital at Prague and Dr Pierre Bonnefoy. (DR)

Given the rank SS-Frw-Oscha during the first promotions of twenty-six French volunteers sent to the training school at Bad Tölz, from 10 January to 4 March 1944, SS-Untersturmführer Léon Gaulthier commanded 2nd Company at the front in Galicia. On 10 August the first two companies were lined up, one facing Pielnia, the other facing the village of Dudyńce, triggering artillery fire which proved fatal to him. Seriously injured, he issued his orders before retreating to the rear. For him, the war was over. This day was particularly deadly for the French, with many sections being put out of action and one even got completely lost and spent two days fighting with a German unit. The nurses were quickly overwhelmed and the reports showed that over sixty were wounded, including many officers (section chiefs and group leaders), as well as several fatalities. (DR)

A document belonging to Léon Gaultier, who in the summer of 1944 will see his destiny turn towards Dudyńce, after the initial engagements by the French troops. (DR)

SS Personalhauptamt II W   Berlin, den 27. Juli 1944
II W II Abt. 3

A k t e n v e r m e r k

Der ehemalige   Leutnant der franz. Armee   (Lt. Patent/Enkling.)
        Teilnehmer des Sonderlehrganges für frz. Offz.
Name :   G a u l t i e r   Vorname: Leon

Geburtsdatum: 1.2.1915   Geburtsort: Bourges

Rangdienstalter in der fremden Wehrmacht:

wird auf Antrag: der Franz. SS Freiw. Sturmbrigade

mit Wirkung vom :   10.3.1944

als: Untersturmführer   ü b e r n o m m e n.

Franz. SS Freiw. Sturmbrigade hat Mitteilung erhalten.

P.d.R.   gez. Dr. K a t z
                SS Brigadeführer und Generalmajor
SS Obersturmführer   der Waffen SS

This photograph allows us to clearly see the national badge of the volunteer on the right. The tricolour badge, without the word 'France' (unlike that of the LVF), was distributed and worn in the spring. According to the directives issued, it had to be less than 5cm down the left sleeve, although it has been seen as far down as the elbow. Wearing the badge caused a level of denial in a significant number of volunteers. They joined the Waffen SS as a result of the complexities of the French Army and to avoid what they disliked about the LVF. They also wanted to be more German than the Germans. Note also that there was no armband issued for the *Franz. SS-Sturmbrigade Nr.8* (*Franz.Nr1*), which for convenience was called *Sturmbrigade 'Frankreich'* by the soldiers. (DR)

A photograph of French volunteers in Galicia, attached to the *18.SS-Freiwilligen-Panzer-Grenadier-Division Horst Wessel*, who were engaged in the 'hottest' areas at the front, where the German lines had cracked. Its commander, SS-Oberführer Trabandt, was greatly relieved at the arrival of this fresh and well equipped battalion.

Proudly waving their national flag, the French SS wave to the official photographer who accompanied them in their baptism of fire in Galicia. The actions of the *Sturmbrigade*'s 1st Battalion resulted in the allocation of several Iron Cross 1st and 2nd Class, many posthumously. Added to the new volunteers from Sennheim were more than 2,000 French Waffen SS who would shortly be sent for training in the new Charlemagne Division. (DR)

In mid-July Marshal Konev's armies began a major offensive on the city of Lviv and southern Poland, breaking the sector held by the German Army group 'North Ukraine', the 1st and 4th Panzer Army. This photograph by the Frenchman SS-Kriegsberichter Briandet, war correspondent to the Kurt Eggers Regiment, shows his compatriots in Galicia at the end of August 1944. It was sent to various press services for eventual publication, although at this time there was no question of it being released in France, which had now seen the majority of its territory freed from German occupation.

SS-Grenadier Guy Eclache was transferred to the *Ersatzkommando Frankreich* on 3 April 1944. Appointed as Waffen SS recruiter in the French town of Grenoble, he formed an armed group of around thirty men on 10 June 1944, which barracked with the local SD. He was later posted to Sennheim on 11 July 1944 as SS-Schütze. After fleeing to Italy in the summer, he was arrested on 27 June 1945 in the Aosta Valley at Caprino-Veronese. (DR)

Chapter Eight

The 33rd Waffen-Grenadier-Division of the SS *Charlemagne* (French No.1)

In the spring of 1944 a command was issued from the OKW to transfer all foreigners serving in the German Army to the Waffen SS. The attack against Hitler on 20 July accelerated this movement, particularly concerning the French. German high command decided to regroup the volunteers into a new SS French brigade, under the command of Colonel Edgard Puaud. The SS-Hauptamt [the administrative office of the SS] decided to bring the 638 French infantry regiment back from Russia. It was disbanded on 10 August 1944 and its members transferred to the Waffen SS. The LVF headquarters at Greifenberg now became the new brigade's headquarters as well as the *Französische SS-Grenadier Ausbildungs und Ersatz-Bataillon* (French SS Grenadier training and reserve Battalion), commanded by SS-Obersturmbannführer Heinrich Hersche who had arrived from Sennheim. The *Sturmbrigade*, whose 1st Battalion had proved itself so valiantly in Galicia, arrived on 5 September and joined 2nd Battalion for training at the 'West-Prussian' SS-Trüppenbüngsplatz. Alongside them, 2,000–2,100 political soldiers were finishing their basic training there, under the command of SS-Oberstumbannführer Paul Gamory-Dubourdeau. In addition there were also men from the *SS-Französische Flakbaterrie*, who had not joined the *Sturmbrigade* in the fighting in Poland, 1,000–1,200 sailors from the Kriegsmarine and *Kriegsmarinewerftpolizei* who had landed at Greifenberg in mid-September, and around 2,000 men who were involved in the *Schutzcommando* and Todt Organisation, the NSKK, the Speer Legion and the Technische Nothilfe, which was part of the German Police. There were also other general German paramilitary units, although some had remained at their original training grounds with the permission of their leaders.

Two regiments were formed, with two battalions each comprised of four companies. The 57th Regiment was predominantly composed of former members of the *Sturmbrigade*, on the orders of Paul Gamory-Dubourdeau. The 58th Regiment was headed by Commander Eugéne Bridoux and contained the ex-Legionnaires. Either for religious reasons (the perceived paganism of the SS), years of combat fatigue, or because they felt the war was definitively lost, a few dozen men categorically refused to be transferred. Taking advantage of this opportunity to start on a clean slate, a purge took place removing 180 of these 'undesirables'. In order to learn the fighting methods of the SS, a number of LVF officers and soldiers were sent on training courses. During their absence, the brigade left its quarters and headed for the *SS-Truppenübungsplatz* at Wildflecken. On 5 November, part of the French state militia had to withdraw from Germany and found itself also being incorporated into the brigade. During the winter of 1944-45, the *Waffen-Grenadier* (no longer the *SS-Grenadier* as those of the *Sturmbrigade* had been called) had to endure particularly harsh training as a result of the snow, the freezing temperatures, lack of equipment and clothes and poor diet. Desertions among the prestigious SS units, such as the Walloon or the Wiking divisions were very common, because their members wanted to join the fighting as soon as possible.

Given the title of 'Division', despite its reduced capacity (more than 7,300 men), the orders to depart for the East by train arrived on 16 February. Integrated with the 11th Army, the first men arrived on 22 February at Hammerstein in Pomerania and gathered in a nearby camp. Sent to the frontlines without any armoured support, heavy weaponry or radio equipment, and with all their assault rifles having been hijacked by another unit, the division's casualties began to pile up. Different companies broke off to fight in isolated groups, with no communication with the rear lines as they were pushed backwards. The survivors retreated to Szczecinek and after this initial engagement, the division had lost around one third of its troops, most of whom were either wounded or evacuated. Five hundred were dead. After regrouping at Białogard, the units were merged together to form a frontline regiment with the freshest and most experienced soldiers, and a reserve regiment with a reduced combat role, due to the fatigue amongst the men. They were sent to protect the retreat of the German troops at the port of Kolberg. Once more the French faced fierce fighting trying to defend the city, forcing them to consider pulling back towards Białogard, which was still held by the Germans. Trapped on a plain south-west of the city, the 3,000 men of the reserve regiment were massacred by Soviet tanks. A few survivors were captured, while others took refuge in the nearby woods. Surrounded for days, the exhausted soldiers now had to finish their war as prisoners, having failed to cross the River Oder. Arriving in Międzyrzecz, in western Poland after a long and painful march, the men of 1st Battalion, who were the only ones left unscathed, managed to succeed in breaking the encirclement of Pomerania. The French regrouped on the outskirts of Anklam and waited for other survivors of the Division.

Stationed at Carpin, the combat units were once more reorganised and resumed their training. On 24 April SS-Brigadeführer Krukenberg, who was now in charge of the French, received a telegram from Hitler's bunker announcing that he was to take up a new position in Berlin and must get there with a French assault battalion as quickly as possible. Having lost three vehicles en route, a French detachment arrived in Berlin, which by now was virtually surrounded by the Red Army. They were attached to the SS Nordland Division, commanded by Waffen-Haupsturmführer Henri Fenet. This division had distinguished itself in urban combat, repulsing many large-scale armoured vehicle attacks using the *Panzerfaüst* [German anti-tank weapon]. The very experienced French soldiers managed to officially take out sixty-two tanks as they gradually retreated to the ever-decreasing German-held zones. On the morning of 2 May, Fenet and his men finally reached Hitler's bunker. They were hoping to find the last kernel of resistance, but instead realised that the battle was all but over. More fighting now commenced in order to avoid being taken prisoner, but one by one the men were arrested by the victorious Soviets, before resistance finally ceased at 3pm.

The remaining men who were still at the barracks at Greifenberg left and joined those at Wildflecken. Here they were divided into various units and separately retreated westwards, where some were subordinated into the *38th SS-Grenadier-Division Nibelungen*. In the end, four members of the division were awarded the Knight's Cross of the Iron Cross.

Colonel Edgard Puaud, photographed here on 26 March 1944, was transferred to the Waffen SS and promoted to Waffen-Oberführer on 1 September. He was there to ensure the operational management of the division, but was hierarchically under the command of SS-Brigadeführer Krukenberg. He was injured in the shoulder at the cemetery in Belgrad during the Pomerania Campaign, and from there issued his final instructions. He remained behind alone as the last of the French SS retreated north-westwards, and as of 5 March 1945 was pronounced missing, presumed dead, due to either his injuries or from the heavy Soviet artillery fire that was bombarding his last-known position. Facing him on the right is Dr Jean-Marie Louis, who was also transferred to the Waffen SS in September. He conducted the medical exams at Greifenberg Camp and offered to declare the legionnaires be discharged as unfit for service, so as to avoid being transferred into the SS.

Before the establishment of a more heterogeneous command unit, Reichsführer Himmler at first created German liaison officers from former members of the LVF who were transferred to the SS. They lived at Leisten and the German officers were required to observe and make reports on the French volunteers, who were far from home and whose families were worried about them. At the head of this inspection of the French SS was Gustav Krukenberg, who had been promoted for the role to the rank of SS-Brigadeführer and Waffen SS Major General on 23 September. Wearing the tricolour badge on his left sleeve, he is seen here in conversation with Waffen-Oberführer Edgard Puaud, who in turn has his back to the head of the Wallonien Division, Léon Degrelle. They are seen here attending the oath swearing ceremony on 12 November 1944. Degrelle, who was surprised to see that the French sang and obeyed their orders in German, was looking for men to join his project of forming a 'Western' Corps made up of French and Walloons, which he would command. SS-Obergruppenführer Gotlob Berger was against the idea and wrote to Himmler about the matter on 16 December, but the idea came to nothing. (DR)

Dr. Gustav Krukenberg

116 685
1 067 635
8-3-88

A file showing the various positions of Dr Gustav Krukenberg before he became head of the French SS inspectorate and for which he was promoted to SS-Brigadeführer and Waffen SS Major General. After hiding at the house of some friends in Berlin, he gave himself up to the Soviet authorities on 12 May 1945, without revealing his rank. He was sentenced to twenty-five years in prison for 'causing damage to the Red Army through his military resistance in Pomerania and Berlin', but was released after eleven years in captivity. (DR)

The unit chaplain, Monseigneur comte Jean de Mayol de Lupé, seen here in Paris on 21 June 1943 wearing his army uniform, accompanied by the former head of the Demessine Battalion. He became a Waffen-Sturmbannführer, but did not take part in the fighting of 1945 and took refuge in a convent before being arrested. The 'path' of the LVF, which was a unit bearing the tricolour flag, under French orders and representing French interests in the East but in a purely German controlled SS unit, led to many legionnaires being confused. Even if the main substance of the anti-Bolshevik struggle remained the same, the initial contracts for signing-up were not respected and a group was formed that intended to abandon them altogether. As only officers had the right to leave, it was the chaplain who tried to convince the volunteers to remain in their positions.

Xavier S had been a legionnaire since 1941 and a sniper for 13th Company during December of that first winter. He was awarded the Iron Cross in May 1944. He returned from Russia in the summer of 1944 after the terrible fighting the LVF had experienced on the Eastern Front and was stationed with his unit at the Greifenberg barracks and at the Saalesch training camp, near Bruss, in the Polish Corridor. He became a junior platoon leader in 9th Company, 58th Regiment, in the new French SS Brigade. As with the great majority of legionnaires, this change in uniform did not alter his intentions. Many continued to wear the national emblem on their right arm (headed by the word 'France') as they had in the army, and in 1944 they also had to wear the SS eagle on their left sleeve. This badge was a regulatory requirement of the *Sturmbrigade*, and for a while was worn at the bottom of the sleeve, according to 1943 regulations.

Future members of the Charlemagne Divison photographed at a time when they were only legionnaires on leave in Versailles, December 1943. Second from the left is Michel De Genouillac, who became an Untersturmführer and was in charge of training 4th Company, 1st Battalion, 58th Regiment, at Bruss, before becoming assistant to Hauptsturmführer Berret in 2nd Battalion. He was taken prisoner in Pomerania. The third soldier, Michel P., left Wildlecken in December 1943 to take up the second part of his officer training at Neveklov in March 1945. He became a member of the Berlin *Sturmbataillon*, after joining his comrades in Carpin that April. The soldier on the right, Antoine N., became an Unterscharführer in 4th Company, 1st Battalion, 58th Regiment, commanding an 80mm mortar unit.

Future members of the Charlemagne Division, here still serving with the LVF and enjoying their departure from Paris on 7 September 1943. They were sent to 5th Company, 2nd Battalion the following year. After the fighting in Pomerania, the soldier on the bottom right will be killed at Hammerstein, the one on the bottom left will be hit in the head by shrapnel, and above him, Robert R. will have his feet amputated.

Former sailor, Robert S., transferred to the Waffen SS with his Kriegsmarine comrades, in September. At the end of the month they were sent to either the barracks at Saales or Waldlager, near Leisten. In Autumn 1944 he was transferred to the Wach-und-Ausb.kp and worked on the brigade's staff, because he was too small. A number of the recruits were promoted to the rank of Waffen-Rottenführer in February [1945], on the orders of the SS-Führungshauptamt. This automatic promotion applied to all those who had served two years in the German or French Armies, and in this case, Robert S. had previously been a Waffen-Sturmann. He left Wildflecken for Pomerania by train on 17 February, at the same time as the train from Bohemia and Moravia arrived carrying the first members of the new company, who had just finished their training. He was awarded the KVK–II [War Merit Cross] on 20 April 1945, as he was the only one at brigade headquarters who did not have one. After the retreat, he surrendered to the English at Bobitz with a dozen or so of the brigade staff. (Coll. R.S.)

The future ordnance officer for the French SS Inspectorate, Heinz Gehring, born 10 February 1917 at Magdeburg. In this photograph he is still a member of the 58th *SS-Standarte* at Cologne/Junkersdorf as he was not transferred to his final posting until early 1945. From 1 December 1944, the unit was called *Waffen-Grenadier Brigade der SS Charlemagne* (*Französische No.1*) and did not become the 33rd *Waffen-Grenadier-Division der SS 'Charlemagne'* (*Französische No.1*) until 10 February 1945. A Grenadier Division was a type of non-motorised division, unlike a Panzergrenadier Division, which had a motorised infantry and its own means of transportation. The name 'Charlemagne', which it had held since October 1944, was a symbol of Franco-German union as this Carolingian emperor had his capital at Aachen (today sometimes called Aix-la-Chapelle). Joan of Arc was also suggested as a possible name, but was not considered 'European' enough. (DR)

Henri Kreis. Former head of the PAK section of the *Sturmbrigade* in Galicia and Kriegkommandant of Radomyśl village, where he was seriously injured when fighting a T34 tank. Once recovered, he became an instructor at the *SS-Panzer-Grenadier-Schule* at Kienschlag. In March 1945 he commanded a reinforcement battalion at Wildflecken, as the division itself had already left for Pomerania. Attached to the *38th Nibelungen Division*, he fought against the Americans in Bavaria with the rank of an Obersturmführer, although in this photograph he is still only an Unterscharführer. (DR)

This document belonged to former LVF member, Jacque Pelletier, who was born on 6 January 1920 and joined up on 24 March 1942. He belonged to the 1st Artillery Group (2nd battery) and was made a corporal in 1st Battalion, before being transferred to 1st Battalion, 58th Regiment. As well as his ID number, blood type and successive ranks, one can also see the signature of Untersturmführer De Genouillac.

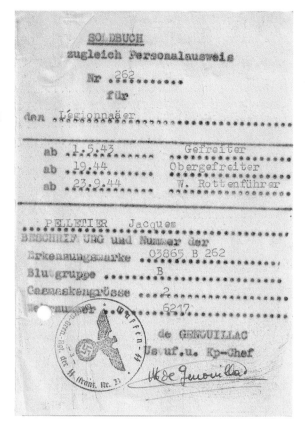

Recognisable by the badge on his left sleeve, a French volunteer is seen here sitting with the public at the Busch Circus in Berlin, 1945. (DR)

On 25 February 1945, Jacques Doriot, the leader of the *Parti Populaire Français* [French Popular Party], which was the most important collaborative political movement, was buried in Mengen. A guard of honour composed of French Waffen SS members from his party surround his coffin. He had been a Waffen-Sturmbannführer since 9 November 1944, although he had not been assigned a unit. (DR)

On the road to Alt-Bork, near Kolberg, these uniformed Frenchmen have been captured by Poles in March 1945. A Polish woman who can speak a little of their language, is trying to find out more about them. The division had broken up and a number of Frenchmen were isolated, sometimes in large groups, and found themselves fighting from wherever they were able to. A hundred or so found themselves at Kolberg and must have headed to Wrocław [Breslau] before the surrender. (Coll.J.Rybicki)

March 1945. These French volunteers are now prisoners and it is clear that they have only just surrendered. They are on the road to Alt-Bork, where the 4th Division of the Polish infantry had its headquarters. They were preparing a grand celebration to mark the fall of the city of Kolberg, which had until recently been held by the Germans. (Coll.J.Rybicki)

Waffen-Untersturmführer Pierre Michel, who went from the LVF to the NSKK in 1942 and then into the Waffen SS on 5 July 1943. He took his loyalty oath at Bad-Tölz after the unit's formation in March 1944, but like all French officers he had to swear it again at Wildflecken. He was sent to the training school in Votice in order to learn how to handle the *Sturmgeschütze* [assault gun]. He did not take part in the Pomerania campaign as his training had not been completed at the time the division moved out to Hammerstein. He rejoined his comrades at Carpin in March 1945, where he once more repeated his oath. Shortly afterwards he led 2nd Company in the *Sturmbataillon*'s assault in Berlin, before receiving serious injuries on 26 April and disappearing somewhere in the Neukölln district. (DR)

Report card for volunteer Pierre Michel following his officer training at SS-Junkerschule, Tölz, from 18 October 1943 to 11 March 1944. (DR)

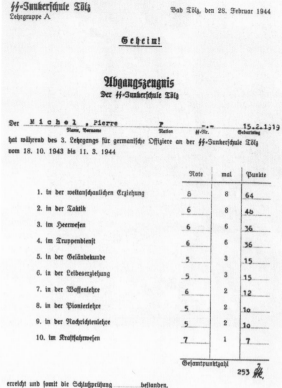

Prisoners of the Charlemagne Division who were executed on 8 May 1945 at Karlstein by their fellow Frenchmen from the 2nd Armoured Division, commanded by General Leclerc, in American uniform and under orders from Paris. In the foreground from left to right are Waffen-Unterscharführer Jean Robert, then Waffen-Obersturmführer Serge Krotoff (of 2nd Bataillon, 57th Regiment), Paul Briffaut in army uniform and Waffen-Untersturmführer Raymond Daffas. The divisional archives had previously been piled onto trucks and destroyed in late April by the Bavarian peasant with whom they had been hidden, as a result of the American advance. (Coll. P. Briffaut)

Left: Waffen-Untersturmführer G., formerly of LVF 10th Company and then 58th Regiment. Along with his section he participated in the dual recovery of a German assault gun and support group from the Russians in Rummelsburg. This photograph was taken in May 1945 at a hospital in Mecklenbourg, where he was a prisoner of the British Army. (DR)

Below: A document dated 14 November 1944 belonging to Dr Pierre Bonnefoy. As can be seen here, he joined the Waffen SS in October 1943 and was currently a Waffen-Obersturmführer in the Charlemagne Division. He was promoted to Waffen-Hauptsurmführer on 30 January 1945 and became the head of the division's medical unit. He was later taken prisoner by the Russians and forced to work in their hospital. (DR)

SS Personalhauptamt II W   Berlin, den ....14.11...1944
II W II Abt. 3

A k t e n v e r m e r k
===========================

Der ehemalige Oberarzt d.Res.der Frz.Armee ....(lt.Patent/XXXXXXX)

Name : B o n n e f o y............... Vorname: ..Pierre..............

Geburtsdatum: 1.8.1908 .... Geburtsort: Belley/Frankreich

Rangdienstalter in der fremden Wehrmacht: 21.7.1937.............

wird auf Antrag: SS-FHA., Amtsgruppe D..............................

mit Wirkung vom : 18.10.1943....................................

als: Waffen - Obersturmführer............. ü b e r n o m m e n.

SS-FHA., Amtsgruppe D und Franz.Brigade der SS haben Mitteilung erhalten.
....

F.d.R.   gez. D r. K a t z

SS Obersturmführer   SS Brigadeführer und Generalmajor
                          der Waffen SS

ℋ-FÜHRUNGSHAUPTAMT
Der Chef des Amtes XI.

An den

Waffen-Standartenjunker

B r a z i e r, Jean

geb.   **4.5.1918**

_____

Ich befördere Sie mit Wirkung vom 1. 9. 1944

zum

WAFFEN - STANDARTENOBERJUNKER

Berlin, den 1. September 1944.

gez.: Dörffler - Schuband

ℋ-Brigadeführer
und Generalmajor der Waffen-ℋ

F. d. R.:

ℋ-Obersturmbannführer
und Lehrgruppen Kdr.

B105.

The appointment of Jean Brazier to Waffen-Standartenoberjunker in early September 1944, following his training at Kienschlag. He had previously completed training at Posen-Treskau from 24 January to 25 February 1944. Promoted to Waffen-Untersturmführer on 9 November, he commanded the *Nachrichtenkompanie*. He became head of 1st Company, 57th Regiment in February 1945 whilst at Kolberg and died in Pomerania. (DR)

Heeresschule
für Btl. - Abt. - Führer

zum Akt Nr. _____
den 10.2.45

Lehrstab   1

VI. gem.   Lehrabteilung

Zur Akte
SS - P H A.

Beurteilung

Anlass der Vorlage : Teilnahme am 20. Lehrgang

in der Zeit vom 3.1. bis 10.2.45

über den

| Ostf. | F e n e t | Henri | SS Gr. Brig. |
| Dienstgrad | Name | Vorname | Charlemagne stelle |

geboren am 11.6.19 letzte Friedensdienststelle Franz. Armee

Laufbahn Res./Kriegsschulanb. R.D.A. (m. Ord. 10.3.44

I. Äussere Erscheinung und Haltung : Mittelgrosse, schlanke Erscheinung,
ordentliche soldatische Haltung, ausreichende Kenntnisse der
deutschen Sprache.

II. Wertung als Persönlichkeit, Truppenführer und Ausbilder : Trotz seiner Jugend
gereifter Charakter, ernstes und gesetztes Wesen, geistig durch-
schnittlich veranlagt, hielt sich vom Unterricht zurück, arbeitete
aber interessiert mit. Taktisches Verständnis ist vorhanden.
Ueberlegte, klare Entschlussfassung. Die Befehlsgebung war knapp
und bestimmt. Erscheint zur Erziehung eines Offz. Korps geeignet.

III. Abschliessendes Urteil :
(gut geeignet, geeignet, noch nicht geeignet, nicht geeignet)

Geeignet.

_____
Unterschrift

Major u. Leiter der Lehrabt.
Dienstgrad und Dienststellung

13. MRZ 1945

Report sheet following a training session in early 1945, for Waffen-Obersturmführer Henri Fenet. As a result of his bravery, he was promoted to captain on 1 March 1945. He participated in the fighting in Berlin as head of the *Sturmbattaillon*. (DR)

Afterword

The experience of those who were taken prisoner differed depending on the nationality of those who captured them. The English and Americans generally handed the French PoWs back to their compatriots in the autumn of 1945, for them to face trial. There were no rules when it came to the Russians. Although scattered in different camps, the majority of French survivors were gathered together at Tambow camp along with men from Alsace-Lorraine who had been conscripted into the Wehrmacht. Following a Franco-Russian agreement signed in Moscow on 29 June 1945, a prisoner 'exchange' took place, although the physical condition of those repatriated was alarming. They were crammed into cattle wagons and it was not until they reached Romania that their condition began to improve. After passing through Odessa and Austria they finally reached France where they were sent to prison. In contrast, those who stayed behind had to suffer the harsh punishments handed out by the 'victors'. Judgements here were much more severe and even included the death penalty. Some volunteers had even switched sides right at the end, and fought the Germans troops despite having previously worn the same uniform as them. Others were forgotten, either choosing exile or service in the French Foreign Legion. Some even left for Indochina, where a new bloody war was beginning for France.